Christianity ADVANCED

The Next Level

Marc Carrier

Warriors Advancing
Rebekah Carrier

We are fighting in a battle; we're warriors in a war.
We will not be intimidated; we know who we fight for.
The One who is on our side is greater by far,
Though those who are against us may think they are.
His power is incredible, His might in working wonders.
He stretches out His mighty hand and evil He plunders.
He hears our intercession, to our prayers He replies
By sending out His hosts of angels, answering our cries.
His angels do His bidding, going out with swords of fire
Breaking barriers, fighting darkness, according to His desire.
We revel in His majesty; we triumph in His glory.
The testimony of His power is our mouths' story.
Oh, our God is so awesome, the Almighty indeed.
We're proud to be in His army, fighting where he'll lead.
We know there is victory in the path that He shows.
Praise continually rises to Him, as His kingdom grows.
No matter what we do, when victory it brings
All the glory goes to Him, the King above all kings.

Contents

Introduction

The Lord has made me a minister and a teacher. However, I am no theologian. I am not nearly as interested in reading and studying as I am in actual field work. I love ministry: leading sinners to repentance and salvation, healing the sick, and delivering people from demons. I love seeing disciples advance in knowledge and power. My greatest passion is mobilizing the saints to action. Because of this, I write.

I do not write to impress you with our exploits and achievements. I don't write to boast or to satisfy my ego. I don't write to see my name in print or to sell books. I write to impart something—to light a fire, to inspire and mobilize to action, to see God glorified as His kingdom comes on earth as it is in Heaven.

As I press on in my calling, every now and again God thrusts me into a new place. He pushes me beyond my comfort zone and advances me to places I had not known existed. Every time this happens, I am compelled to share what He has revealed and done in me, in hopes that the revelation will bear the same fruit in others that it has in my ministry. Now is one of those times.

My book *Christianity Unleashed* was written after God brought me, and other members of our mission here in Kenya, to repentance for neglecting the power and leading of the Holy Spirit in our lives and ministry. As we walked out that repentance, God poured Himself upon us in presence and power and unleashed signs and wonders. *Christianity Unleashed* was written to *unleash* captive saints from seen and unseen bondages, and to *unleash* a flood of laborers into the field preaching, healing, and expelling demons.

Like *Christianity Unleashed*, *Christianity Advanced* also has a double meaning in hopes of accomplishing a dual purpose. *Christianity Advanced* is about taking the saints to the next level, advancing beyond the elementary teachings as we see in the book of Hebrews:

Therefore leaving the elementary teaching about the Christ, let us press on to maturity, not laying again a foundation of repentance from dead works and of faith toward God, of instruction about washings and laying on of hands, and the resurrection of the dead and eternal judgment. And this we will do, if God permits. (Hebrews 6:1-3)

Here the writer implores the reader to move beyond the fundamentals of Christ: repentance, faith, the filling of the Holy Spirit (laying on of hands), and life eternal. There is another level.

The second meaning of *Christianity Advanced* is less obvious. As we personally take our walk to the next level, we also need to advance Christianity itself, moving from *defensive* to *offensive* warfare: reading the enemy's mail, thwarting his plans, and advancing our front lines into the enemy's camp to plunder his forces.

With the objective revealed, let me now explain the ground rules that you should keep in mind as you read this book. This is not a theological work. I did not learn these gifts or how to perform front-line work by reading books. I stepped out in obedience and God showed up in power. Therefore, this is a testimonial, not a dissertation. If you require lots of Biblical evidence for these advanced subjects (for which the Bible actually offers little supporting material), put this book down and stick to the elementary teachings. However, if you are ready to advance your walk and your ministry, I recommend you not only read this book, but apply as much as you can.

Marc Carrier

Where We Left Off

For the benefit of those of you who are not familiar with my testimony, I am a missionary serving in Kenya with my wife and now eleven children. I first visited Kenya in 2009 and moved there with the family early in 2012. The first several years of the mission were riddled with exciting advances followed by failures and disappointments. The constant betrayals I experienced really took their toll on me emotionally and, therefore, spiritually. This reality, as well as my association with a persuasion of Christianity that really did not walk in the power and leading of the Holy Spirit, led me to the point that I was operating almost entirely devoid of the living Spirit. It looked like we were doing all the right things in the mission, but what we had was a poor substitute for the vibrant realities recorded in the book of Acts.

It all came to a screeching halt early in 2017, when God got my attention through His supernatural intervention. He started demonstrating His reality through prophesies, healings, and deliverances during all-night prayer meetings. After an extended fast, the Lord ministered radical change in my own life through my repentance for neglecting the power and leading of the Holy Spirit. Following this revelation, I corrected my failures in the mission by revisiting the churches and introducing the brethren to Spirit baptism and the gifts of the Spirit. And God showed up.

During this time of recommitment and renewal, we experienced many miraculous healings and as many demonic manifestations and deliverances. Prophecies also increased exponentially. These were exciting times, since such events had previously been few and far between. Yet with these experiences came as many questions as answers. We understood little about demons and their functions and characteristics. Healing was likewise new to us.

Through trial and error we navigated through this uncharted territory and the Lord took the mission to new levels. However, as much as we saw the presence of God, we were disturbed to see alongside of it the demonic oppression among our people. We would deliver someone, and weeks later see the same presence. We received prophetic words about witchcraft attacks and had to learn how to deal with those. At the time, we had no idea what the inter-relation was between witchcraft and demons. All we knew was that unseen powers of evil were fighting against us, and we were nearly blind to their presence and activity. We needed the Lord to open our eyes.

Discerning of Spirits Activated

At one of our regular fasting meetings, a demon fully manifested in the same woman again, a member of one of our village house churches. She had asked for prayer for a rash; when I began praying she kicked and screamed and fell backwards with a loud *thud* as her head hit the cement floor. I wondered if she could die. But instead she kept kicking and screaming as I commanded the demon to leave her. After a couple minutes of intense and forceful commands, she grew calm and regained her senses. Amazingly, her rash was completely gone.

At another such prayer meeting we received a prophetic revelation that there was a witchcraft curse against our compound yet again. My oldest son, seeing some suspicious activity outside his gate one evening, later inspected near one post and uncovered a small baggie containing burnt leaves mixed with blood. (An object is often used to place a curse in ritual witchcraft.)

Commonplace events like these made me feel powerless to defend myself, my family, and the disciples, as I worked to advance the mission. I knew we needed tools. We were blind and the enemy had the upper hand. We always seemed to be one step behind his schemes.

A visitor to our prayer meetings from another ministry prophetically declared to me that the Lord would give me "a screen" to see what was inside people—in biblical terms, the gift of discerning of spirits. He said it would be good, and bad: good that we would know what we were facing, and bad that I would see some things I did not want to know about in people I trusted.

As soon as I heard this prophecy, I earnestly sought the gift through unrelenting petition to the Lord. Seeing repeated demonic manifestations in supposed brethren and the constant barrage of attacks from witchcraft, I was desperate for eyes to see. We were in the process of planning a visit to America for the first time since moving to Kenya. During that trip, as the rest of the family returned to Kenya, my sixteen-year-old son and I were scheduled to travel to several places to minister to people. I knew I would need these tools for effective ministry, and I eagerly anticipated their activation. But to my great disappointment, it didn't happen.

We continued to press forward upon my return to Kenya, battling both demons and curses without a clear understanding of what we were doing. It was mighty discouraging at times. We relied on resources and methods published by other ministers on deliverance, but we later learned that some of the methods we adopted were not good at all. Being blind to what was going on in the spiritual realm, we relied nearly exclusively on information we obtained from the demons themselves. It was all we had and all we knew that had proven effective in the fight. As well, the benefits of deliverance were not always permanent. And nothing in our limited research told us how to defeat witchcraft. We knew we were still missing lots of important details.

One day, a few of our gifted women expressed their opinion that the leading men in the mission would benefit from concerted prayer for activation of spiritual gifts. I suggested a fasting meeting for the following week. During that meeting, one woman brought a word to the group: *if someone can't keep a secret, God will not give them revelations.* That word pierced me deeply, because a couple years prior a brother had told me that the Lord had warned him not to share some things with me for just that reason. The distant memory immediately came to my recollection. In response, I repented completely, recognizing that this was the only reason God had delayed in activating the gift of discerning of spirits in me. Then I simply told God, *I don't care who You give the gift to—it can be anyone in our mission—it doesn't have to be me.* We just could no longer continue working blindly. We needed help and *now.*

Two days later, while preparing to do a deliverance for a young man in our mission, my wife, Cindy, discerned the spirits influencing him, even in his absence. We asked about his wife and likewise received reports. (Up until this time, we always had to be with the person, and we would resort to asking the demons their names and primary works.) It was at that moment we recognized that it was indeed the Holy Spirit providing the information, and not demons. Something had changed.

That night at an all-night prayer meeting, during our

time of repentance, the Lord revealed to me several small things I was doing in my life that were displeasing to him. I repented deeply. As these items were revealed, I did not delay or equivocate; I simply renounced the things I had been doing. God was clearly preparing me for more.

Another fasting meeting began the following Wednesday. Cindy did not attend due to pregnancy, but eight others came. In just that week Cindy's gift of discerning of spirits had greatly increased and we began testing how to use it effectively. Yet she was still holding back the details of what she had been personally experiencing. Little did I know, I would soon participate in similar experiences myself.

On the second day of fasting I woke up at 3:30 AM to the sound of a voice speaking to me; not audibly, but rather in my head. It was loud and pronounced, completely out of my control, and free from influence from my own thoughts. In fact, the voice was actually distinct from my own mind's voice. I forget the first discourse, but I recall asking if it was God. He replied that it was indeed the Holy Spirit. That precipitated a literal three-hour conversation, with me asking the Lord every single question I could think of: about my life, about the Bible, about the future. It was me alone with God like Moses on the mountain, an unfathomably intimate experience that I never wanted to end. There I was with my God—He and I alone, talking like a son and his dad. He answered just about everything I asked, with only an occasional, "That's not for you to know." My only fear was that this would stop—that this was only a one-time experience that would end. I trembled at the thought.

In our conversation I asked Him what I was experiencing. He responded that it was the gift of knowledge. I then asked if Cindy had this, too. He answered, "Yes." I now couldn't wait to talk to her. At 6:30 AM, when I knew she would be awake, I called at once. I asked her if God was talking to her in her head. She answered, "Yes."

I asked her why she hadn't told me. She said she feared I would think she was crazy (a reasonable conclusion, actually). But now that the Lord had activated the gift in me as well, I knew it was legitimate.

In the following days and weeks we were able to fine-tune these gifts to leverage their usefulness for advancing our mission. Though the voice of the Lord wasn't as "loud" after that first experience, it never desisted.

Through direct conversation with the Holy Spirit, and now with Cindy and I being able to confirm our messages with each other, we were permitted to inquire into all sorts of areas of need in our ministry. Likewise, discerning of spirits became precise when we worked in unison. With me on lead, asking the Lord for insight, and with Cindy focusing on hearing His voice, we could solicit spiritual information on demand, with definitive answers given. Yet there were limitations, or rules to how it worked, that we learned as we went along.

The process relies on authority (more on that later) and

is predicated on faith; this is my contribution to the equation. It demands, on Cindy's part, what I would describe as perfected humility (which Cindy hates me saying). This prevents deceptive spirits from interjecting and allows for clear insight. We then can identify demons, curses, spirits, and even spiritual gifts, manifestations, and calls. We also occasionally receive specific words of knowledge as well. The discerning of spirits is not a visual seeing but rather, a spiritual understanding.

Once we learned how the gifts operated and fine-tuned how to use them, we proceeded to clean up our fellowship thoroughly. During our corporate Saturday afternoon prayer meetings, Cindy and I made ourselves privately available for anyone wanting personal prayer. There were always long lines. In these meetings we focused on deliverance, but very often as demons were expelled and curses were cancelled, healings occurred. With the healings came larger crowds, some people from other churches (and even non-believers) traveling great distances for prayer. Many were saved and several churches were planted directly as a result of the activation of these gifts.

One such event was when Michelle was very sick to the point of death. She had not been able to eat normally for several weeks and had little strength left. She went to multiple doctors but saw no improvement in her condition. She resigned to the fact that she could die. One day, she collapsed on the path near her home, weak but still conscious. Our sister, Catherine, happened by and told Michelle she needed to come to our prayer meeting because people were healed there regularly. Catherine helped her travel to the meeting. After the time of teaching, Cindy and I went to our private room. Michelle was just one person in a long line of people that we welcomed. We defeated the demons and witchcraft we saw and she went on her way; we learned nothing of her specific backstory. I don't even think she told us at that time that she was completely healed! Her testimony of healing eventually led to dozens of people being saved (including her entire family) and many more healed in her distant village. A church meets in the house of her brother-in-law to this day.

I started reporting on Facebook the amazing developments we were now seeing routinely in Kenya. It was with some trepidation that I discussed the spiritual gifts that we were relying on for the work, as part of me expected disbelief or criticism and I didn't want to enter into debate or conflict because of it. Somewhat to my surprise, I didn't get much negative response but, rather, a number of sincere prayer requests.

At first we scheduled calls at random when all parties were available. However, as word-of-mouth brought an increase in prayer appointments, we knew we needed to get organized. We started scheduling a single call daily, at 6:30 AM Kenya time, and the backlog of appointments was consistently over a month out. It took us about seven months of daily calls before we finally got ahead; we continued (and still schedule) the calls for anyone who gets in touch and requests one.

When the gifts first activated we quickly saw the incredible power of knowing the enemy's plans and works. Cindy and I would pray for insane beggars on the streets and see them restored to sanity. Some remained sane, and some we saw relapse over time. Either way, the awesome power of God and His glory were evident. Every experience was a learning opportunity.

The week following the activation of the gifts of knowledge and discerning of spirits in Cindy and me, we had to travel to Nairobi with my son and his wife to witness their formal wedding ceremony at the Registrar of marriages. While in the waiting room, I told them to watch a particular man when I approached him. He had a demon who knew that I could see him, and he was terribly frightened. As I neared him, he visibly trembled. I just smiled.

During the long travel to and from Nairobi, Cindy and I could identify every principality as we traveled and we discerned when they changed. It was a new and strange experience, indeed. We were amazed at God's power.

During our stay in Nairobi, God had activated other gifts in me, including faith. On the way back home, we expected to be disturbed by police (as usual) during routine traffic stops. Each time we approached a police checkpoint, I would pray very specifically, play-by-play, exactly what I wanted the officers to do. And to our amazement, they did what I prayed at all five or six checkpoints: "Get distracted, look away, look at your phone, walk away, stop the truck instead of me." We made it all the way from Nairobi to my home without being stopped once—a first for such a long trip. We knew we had advanced to a completely new place spiritually.

Discerning of Spirits Essentials

The gift of discerning of spirits is given by the Holy Spirit to assist the church in identifying spiritual attributes or entities which are otherwise invisible and often indiscernible in the natural. It is quite valuable in the work of deliverance. There is precious little in Scripture about how the gift operates and how it is supposed to be used. Therefore, I write from our experiences and you can glean what you wish from my testimony.

Just a note as we begin: when I refer to a person undergoing deliverance, I will most often refer to them as the "victim." This seems to me a loaded term, as oftentimes people are responsible for a lot of the things that plague them and I don't want to put all the blame on the demonic realm. However, for lack of a better term, "victim" is what I will typically use going forward.

The discerning of spirits functions quite differently for Cindy and me independently than it does when we work together. Individually, as we pray for someone we receive insight into that person's spiritual needs. It's really a thought or a "knowing" that we then convert to an actual word. We typically discern the primary work or main attribute that best describes a demon. Rarely but occasionally, the thought will be of a name. The insight prompts us to pray specifically for deliverance from said demon. In some cases more information, such as a detailed description of what is disturbing the person or a history of the situation, comes via a word of knowledge. That provides additional direction for the deliverance, such as the victim repenting of specific sin, forgiving someone, releasing a situation, renouncing something, or anything else necessary to release them from demonic influence. The information is usually limited, and very specific to the need of the moment.

In contrast, when we work together, we have the unique ability to inquire concerning everything attacking a victim spiritually: demons, curses, and spirits. We are able to see all this with precision whenever we pray, as long as we have authority or else permission to inquire.

The cooperative function works this way: I inquire, and Cindy receives the insight. Alone, we each can receive bits and pieces. But together, we get it all. Our method has been optimized over the course of conducting several hundred deliverances. Each and every step we take during deliverance has a specific purpose, many added to our repertoire as a result of something we learned in the field by something going wrong. We borrowed precious little from other deliverance ministers. You are certainly free to accept or reject what we offer here. However, I can confidently say that what we do is field-proven to be consistently very effective.

We start by binding the strong man. This is the ruling fallen angel, from whom orders ultimately originate. When we attack lowly demons, an unhindered strong man can send reinforcements and disseminate attack orders to a larger force. Binding him limits his abilities and his awareness concerning the target you are praying for. It does nothing to limit his abilities or involvement in works outside the prayer focus.

We then bind spirits of deception and confusion. Demons with these two responsibilities are very common. They are the two types of demons who will typically be tasked with interfering with the use of revelatory gifts, including word of knowledge and discerning of spirits. If they have free reign to attack the victim being prayed for or the deliverance minister(s), they can influence the session to produce anywhere from a completely false report, to a just-slightly-twisted report. Binding them blocks their influence.

Next we declare that only the Holy Spirit can speak, and we ask Him to provide a complete report with nothing hidden. This is because demons will frequently try to remain anonymous so that they will not be expelled and they can continue their work. Calling them out from the beginning and asking for the Holy Spirit's assistance in revealing everything demonstrates to the spiritual forces of evil that we mean business.

Next, we identify the demonic team attacking the victim. Demons work in groups, functioning under various permissions with many works and effects. We ask who the leader of the group is; he is labeled the "prince," because he is the ruler of a little team or

kingdom. Then we ask who is in his kingdom. One by one, we identify them by their primary work.
Besides demons and curses, we can also identify spirits (including the gatekeeper, or the first influencer that opened the door to others), soul wounds or emotional trauma requiring healing, and even spiritual gifts—all with the same gift of discerning of spirits.

I'm sure others may use terminology different from mine, so let me clarify a bit. Angels and demons are often generically referred to as "spirits," and that is an accurate description, but in our experience a spirit is a distinct entity. A "spirit" describes a non-personal, invisible object placed in us to perform an ongoing work. As the Holy Spirit described it to me, it is like kryptonite for Superman. Kryptonite does not have a mind of its own, but it does perform the work of sapping Superman's strength. It was placed there by a living being who had a specific plan. Therefore, as an example, a person can be attacked by a demon of lust, or they can have a spirit of lust. A demon of lust would actively work to bring about specific effects, whereas a spirit of lust may only cause unwanted images to be called to mind involuntarily. A spirit has no mind of its own, but rather is programmed to accomplish work set forth by the demon who placed it there. It also serves as a beacon for the spiritual forces of evil to indicate a weakness or provide a gateway.

After going through the process of deliverance from all affecting spirits, we pray through any healing (physical or emotional) that seems necessary and finish with a prayer for the Holy Spirit to fill up any places left empty by now-departed competing spirits. At that time, I will ask for identification of spiritual "gifts." (I put the word "gifts" in quotes for a reason—because it's not simply the gifts, but rather the manifestations of the Holy Spirit in a person's life.) As in 1 Corinthians 12, there are "gifts," "ministries," and "effects" which encompass the full manifestation of the Holy Spirit. We have identified numerous manifestations not found in the main lists of gifts in Scripture. Some include praise and worship, prayer and intercession, prophetic dreams and visions, music, and deliverance ministry, among others. The Holy Spirit can operate in many more ways than Paul listed in his letters; these lists were never meant to be exhaustive.

This is a brief description of how we use discerning of spirits in the process of deliverance, but let me offer some insight into the gift itself—at least, how it has worked for us. The discerning of spirits comes not as a vision, not an audible (mind's voice) word, but rather as a thought impression that must be translated into words. It takes practice and discipline to quiet all distractions and discern the reports with precision. This is why our team effort has proven so effective. I take the lead and pray, engage the victim, take notes, and perform the actual deliverance, while Cindy just focuses on the one task of discernment. She blocks everything out, closes her eyes, and just listens.

During active ministry, I am personally not capable of quieting myself sufficiently to differentiate between my own thoughts and the messages from the Holy Spirit. And Cindy can't both lead and hear, either. So I believe it takes a team to seek and hear the full report in real-time with precision.

I think it's important here to elaborate on ensuring the validity of the information discerned. We learned with the revelatory gifts that humility is imperative, as is emotional stability. Pride is the gateway to deceiving spirits. Often, mental or emotional instability will permit a spirit of confusion. These types of demons can influence the reports, sometimes subtly and other times more obviously. We have seen powerfully gifted people reporting falsely before. Sometimes the information provided is in conflict with God's Word, and other times it conflicts with known facts. Occasionally the Spirit will simply provide a member of the group with a feeling that something is "off." With deliverance, the gifts can resume with accuracy. This is why the Lord admonishes us to test the spirits and hold onto what is good. Yet another advantage of operating as a team or group is that there are more such checks and balances. And remember, anything brought to you by another person should confirm what you already know, or you should have an "inner witness" to its validity.

With all the revelatory gifts, adequate faith is required to receive the report. It's not blind faith, as in accepting things regardless of their truthfulness. It's a built up or acquired faith developed by testing the reports repeatedly by asking the victim if the things you heard by the Spirit match their experience. After numerous times of validating the accuracy of reports, you come to believe and simply expect accurate reports. Likewise, with more practice, the discerning becomes easier.

We have found that learning as little as possible about the prayer target helps to hone the gift of discerning of spirits and the accompanying word of knowledge. This is because if we know background information, it is possible to presume things from the mind rather than discern them from the Spirit. I know I sometimes struggle with separating my own thoughts from those of the Holy Spirit. I am always thinking and have a very difficult time quieting myself sufficiently to hear the Lord's voice accurately. Again, this is why I lead the prayer sessions and let Cindy discern. She has trained herself to quiet her own thoughts and simply listen to the messaging of the Holy Spirit in response to my prayers of inquiry.

With discerning of spirits, we do not see sin. However, we identify demons and spirits whose primary work may indeed reflect a particular sin (i.e., lust or anger). Therefore, it is a very safe assumption that someone with a demon of lust struggles with sins associated with lust. On the other hand, someone with a spirit of lust typically has repented and made strides to overcome overt sin, but they may still have ongoing problems— with thought life, for example. In such a case, an active demon has moved on to more productive targets and left a spirit behind to keep the victim struggling.

When demons are sent because of generational curses, occasionally the victim will not recognize it at all in themselves, but they may be aware of issues in previous generations. In such cases, a demon is simply following them because of a curse and may manifest later in life or with the next generation (as either a sin problem or health issue, for example). Kind of like a recessive genetic disease, the trait is there, yet not evident; however, it can manifest at another time.

Discerning of spirits is authority-based. We learned through practice that I have authority to inquire about any disciples under my watch. (Even though I have the authority, I still need Cindy for the gift to work with precision). This includes people I have discipled, even many years ago, that still ask me for counsel or respect me as a spiritual advisor. Disciples in fellowship do not need to be present, nor do they need to grant us specific permission. We can't inquire about people outside this sphere of influence, even those who are (through the process of church discipline) put out of fellowship or who voluntarily leave. Outside our fellowships we can only pray for people who grant us permission. Then we can pray in person, by email, phone, messenger, or WhatsApp, and see everything.

Because of the authority paradigm, we can see a wife through her husband (that is, if the marriage is amicable). We can see minor children through either parent, even if they are adopted. If we beg God, we can get limited information on people outside the chain of authority, but we very rarely discern any spirits or demons associated with sin. We will only see curses and demons where the prayer target is simply a victim of those things and where deliverance would be for their edification. Information is usually only provided if we legitimately have a need to know, for the victim's benefit and not just out of personal curiosity.

Here is a sample prayer for using the gift of discerning of spirits in deliverance:

I bind the strong man. I bind the spirits of deception and confusion. Only the Holy Spirit may speak. Give me a full report, full disclosure, nothing hidden, nothing secret. Who is the prince? (We get an answer and write it down). Who's in his kingdom? (We get an answer and write it down.) Who else? (We write down any additional revelation.) Are there any curses—generational, curse of words, or witchcraft? (If yes, we list each type of curse by the demon/spirit identifications.) Which are demons and which are spirits? (We write down demon or spirit by their identifiers, knowing the prince is always a demon, and the last one we receive is always the gatekeeper, a spirit.)

As I've already said, I can't speak for how these gifts work for others. Therefore, I am simply testifying to how they work for us, in hopes that the information may benefit others in honing in their skills in the discerning of spirits.

Evil Spirits and Their Works

So far we have identified three forms of evil spirits: fallen angels, demons, and impersonal spirits. Fallen angels are created spiritual beings whose power and authority is greater than humans'. Some of these angels transgressed by taking women and have been condemned to the pit. The others roam freely, Satan being the ruling angel over them.

The Ante-Nicene church concurred that the angels who rebelled against God were rogue spirits distinct from the demons, with greater power and authority. They also unanimously believed that demons were the disembodied spirits of the Nephilim (the giants cited in Genesis chapter 6). This understanding is referred to in the Book of Enoch, which was widely accepted as accurate in its original form by the early church. I always considered this account reasonable, with little reason to doubt their interpretation. And the Scriptures concur that angels are of greater authority than humans, even the saints, and that the demons are beneath the saints in authority. Our work in deliverance with discerning of spirits and word of knowledge has only confirmed this understanding.

I believe that the work of deliverance has been ignored for too long by the modern church and many sincere Christians are left in unnecessary bondage. It is important to understand the dynamic in the battle that we fight against the spiritual forces of evil. As I discuss this paradigm further, I do so with some trepidation;

whenever others present information that was acquired through special revelation, I am suspicious by default. However, test the spirits and understand that the theory I present is secondary to the application: deliverance from all spiritual oppression. What we have discerned of the spiritual realm comes from performing over a thousand successful deliverances; our understanding maps precisely to that of the early church witness and presents no conflicts with Scripture.

Demons were once living beings—half-breeds from the procreation of fallen angels and human women that they deceived (see Genesis 6:4). The angels were condemned to the pit for their transgression. Their progeny were not immediately punished like their angelic fathers, nor could they be sent to Hades, the place of the human dead. Instead, they were condemned to roam the earth, with no opportunity for redemption, until their final judgment at the end of the age.

Thus, these spirits of the giants are now soldiers of the devil and his angels. Their primary role is to prevent humans from changing allegiance from Satan, sin, and the world to God and His kingdom through Christ Jesus. Since they have no opportunity for redemption, they work to block humans from achieving that goal. They hate us because God showed us His great mercy by offering redemption through Jesus Christ, an opportunity that they were denied. They are profoundly jealous and bitter of our favored status, so they aim to punish us for it.

The demons' secondary goal is to distract us from the Lord's service, to render us unproductive and ineffective at advancing God's kingdom. This can be achieved through both curses and blessings—whatever it takes to keep our eyes off the kingdom. Through sicknesses, emotional trauma, mental disorders, distractions, addictions, conflicts, disturbances, and even material blessings, the spiritual forces of evil subvert God's plan for our lives. They are opportunists and attack the areas of greatest weakness and vulnerability in our lives.

In conversations about the demonic realm, the terms *possession* and *oppression* are hotly debated. Demonic possession has a generally accepted meaning of having one's faculties dominated by an alternative influence. However, this term is seldom used in Scripture and such a case is equally rare in our experiences with deliverance. Instead, we see demonic attacks, or what some would refer to as oppression.

But let's skip the theology and stick to the practical. Truthfully, everyone is under attack; the demonic realm doesn't want any of us to be saved or to advance in our faith, so they fight us at every opportunity. We have never seen someone we ministered to *not* under attack, unless they were recently freed through deliverance or they consistently and proactively fight the spiritual attacks in prayer. At the same time, we very rarely see indwelling demons (what people term possession) in professing Christians. This fact offers little solace, however, when we consider that demons have the same impact in the lives of their victims whether they are indwelling or attacking from the outside. The debate of *possession* versus *oppression* is only a subject of theological interest; practically, it matters little as regards demons' potential influence on people's lives.

The spiritual realm operates like a military with a chain of command, issuing orders down the chain to accomplish its purposes. Their purpose is ultimately to outnumber their enemies: God, the loyal angels, and the saints. Satan and the fallen angels are interpreted as having far fewer numbers than the faithful angels. However, add in the demons and all of sinful humanity, and their forces are formidable.

God, on the other hand, is recruiting (through us saints) defectors from Satan's ranks. His goal, of course, is for humans to repent and change their allegiance from Satan to God, from darkness to light, the kingdom of the world to the kingdom of God. Satan and his army work diligently to thwart that effort. We all know it's a hopeless venture; we know how it all ends. However, the demonic realm will not relent until their final and unequivocal defeat. I have spoken to Satanists who actually believe that they can, and will, win. They hope in vain, but they must try.

The dark spiritual realm, much like the armies of the world, operates by rules and authority. Interestingly, we discovered that many of the demons don't like each other or their ranking overlords. They operate by command and control, and instill fear even into each other.

Demons exercise their work on humans mostly through stealth. Unsuspecting victims typically believe that their circumstances are the result of random events— simply human experience. After all, as Solomon wrote in Ecclesiastes, don't time and chance overtake us all? However, many (if not most) common emotional, physical, and psychological challenges are actually demonic attacks. Although not every issue in life is because of a demon, more of them are than people assume.

Demons need permission in order to influence humanity, so they take advantage of any weakness presented to them in order to gain access. The initial spirit that opens the door to attack nearly always enters because of some form of emotional trauma. The four most common gatekeepers we see are fear, insecurity, rejection, and unforgiveness. Other attacks are based on sins and curses. Once the door is open, the demonic realm has free reign to take advantage and attack, often in insidious ways.

Any unrepented sin grants demons permission to attack. Though not obvious to most, the gatekeepers mentioned (fear, insecurity, unforgiveness, and rejection) are actually sin, since Jesus said he would never leave nor forsake us; He commanded us not to fear, not to worry, and to forgive. But these are softer sins, rarely recognized as such. That is probably why we see them used as points of access so frequently.

When we do deliverance, the final step is to confirm that the demons and spirits are gone and have closed any of these open doors. If they don't go, or if the gate isn't shut, the Lord will reveal that and even provide the reason why. (Sometimes repentance, renouncing, or forgiving/releasing someone are necessary to remove any permissions the demons feel they have.) Cindy detects the closing of the gate as an in-the-mind audible shutting sound. The Lord may then reveal soul wounds resulting from emotional trauma that require healing. This healing is necessary to prevent a re-opening of the gate and a recurring attack. I'll go into further detail on these aspects of deliverance later.

As I've said previously, spirits are not persons. They are spiritual objects placed by a personal demon to accomplish a specific work. Gatekeepers, or the open door to demonic attack, are always spirits. During deliverance they behave exactly like demons, as far as leaving on command.

With a background now in how the demonic realm is organized and how the rank-and-file function, we'll move on to the actual process of deliverance—how to take authority over and remove them.

Deliverance Essentials

It is important to know that demons attack everyone, saint or sinner. A single demon can influence, or oppress, numerous victims at once; they are not spatially limited. It is actually not very common to find indwelling demons, or what is referred to as demon possession. As I said previously, it is extremely rare to find a saint with an indwelling demon; we've only seen it in the backslidden or apostate. For all intents and purposes, however, demons can have the same influence on the saved and the unsaved; that's why deliverance is so vital.

There is a misconception that once we are saved, deliverance is automatic. This is not true, and it is why so many suffer under continued oppression. Certainly, demons no longer have authority over us once our sins are forgiven through Christ. However, they don't desist or leave unless compelled (commanded) to do so. Just like with physical sicknesses and diseases, the saints have all authority over them in Christ. Yet that authority must be exercised through prayers or commands of healing. Sick sinners do not emerge from the baptismal waters as healed saints automatically. Neither are demons repelled by baptismal waters. They must be commanded to leave in the Name of Jesus Christ. Absent deliberate deliverance, their influence remains.

Another serious misconception is that once someone is saved, demons and the powers of darkness can no longer hurt them. This is also not true. If we have unhealed emotional wounds, come under a curse, or fall back into sin, they are granted access for influence. They can even attack absent an open door; though their effects will be minimal, they can (and should) still be commanded to cease and desist their efforts.

Although most demons are not indwelling, during deliverance they present themselves as commanded in order to be expelled. Thus, the victim often feels or manifests the demons' departure as if they were indwelling. If this dynamic is not understood, it can lead to confusion, or even anxiety, in a sincere Christian going through the deliverance process.

Since the authority to expel demons rests with our being in Christ, it is unwise to deliver the unsaved unless it is a precursor to baptism following their repentance. Any freedom experienced by an unsaved person will quickly be reversed (see Matthew 12:43-45).

For the unsaved, we bind demons, but don't expel. Binding demons or angels temporarily constrains their abilities in a specific way. They are not permanently put out of commission, but only for a time—perhaps a day or two. They are not limited in all their functions, but only according to the prayer request. Binding angels can keep them from interfering with the work of deliverance, or they can be bound from issuing attack orders down the chain of command. Binding demons can blind them to your activities or limit their influence over particular situations. Remember, we have only been given authority over demons, not over angels. We cannot defeat angels or send them to the pit; we simply bind them.

In practice, when we bind, it is the Lord who actually executes the work through the dispatching of angels. We can command demons, but the Lord commands His host to fight evil angels at a higher level. We are not privy to all the details; we just rest assured that when we bind angels or demons, they will not interfere with our work thanks to the Lord's assistance. Therefore, with unsaved or uncooperative victims, binding is the best option, and we may ask the Lord to command His host to fight for us in other ways.

Demons attack for a number of reasons. No matter how they gain entry, however, the saints have complete authority over them through the Name of Jesus Christ. Deliverance, or exorcism, exercises that authority in order to free victims from demonic attack. In order to expel demons, we must first break any permissions they have: sin, curses, or an open door from emotional trauma. Demons can technically be expelled without breaking their permissions, but if this step is omitted there will almost certainly be a recurring attack.

First and foremost, demons are invited because of sin. We can't blame demons for our misbehaviors; they are, in fact, invited into our lives *by* those misbehaviors. You could say that demons simply exacerbate problems that already exist. The victim must repent of any sin that permits demonic attack in order for the demons to leave upon command. Though they can be forced to go with persistence or appeal for angelic assistance, it is futile. Continued sin will simply welcome a recurring attack from a demon of identical work assignment.

The second reason they attack is curses. We have identified three common types of curses: witchcraft, generational curses, and spoken curses. Witchcraft is calling upon demons to perform an activity (either positive or negative), and is typically directed towards a person or their property. The demons are usually urged to action through a ritual that pleases or appeases them. Once the orders are issued and the victim targeted, the demons will persist in their attack unless the orders are canceled. It is cancelled through prayers such as "I break, chop, cancel, and end any curses against the victim or his property in Jesus' Name." This will end the curse. However, there are two more steps. First, the demon activated by the curse still needs to be expelled; ending the curse is not the same as deliverance. Second, if an object was used in sending the curse, then the object needs to be deactivated. For example, if someone did a ritual and blood and leaves were placed at a particular location to bring sickness or death, the curse can be canceled and demons of sickness and death expelled. However, if a physical object remains, it can act as a beacon (visible in the spiritual realm) which can leave a door open for ongoing demonic attack. Therefore, we must ask the Holy Spirit or angels to find and burn the objects, annulling their work.

A generational curse is typically demons permitted or assigned to follow the lineage of unrepentant victims after they die. This type of curse remains active through generations unless broken. Though the same demons often disturb multiple members of a family, this is unique in that the orders remain even if demons are expelled. That means even following deliverance, if the curse is not cancelled, new demons with identical tasking will resume the work. Again, the curse serves as a beacon of sorts, attracting demons with a particular area of concentration. To break a generational curse, simply renounce it and declare it cancelled in Jesus' Name.

The third form of common curse is a curse of words, or spoken curse. I never fully recognized the power of our words before I started doing deliverance. We have power to bless and to curse; when we curse, we send demons to execute a work. Although anyone can issue a curse of words, it is specifically people in authority who are most likely to unleash a demon against someone that they influence. A curse of this type is not from a ritual or by specific words, but may be spoken idly or unawares. For example, "Their marriage will never succeed," or "You are a loser; you'll never amount to anything!" These simple statements can invite demons of division or defeat. We parents, in particular, have to be very careful what we say about and to our children. Our words can easily become self-fulfilling prophesies through demonic agency.

Demons typically work in groups to optimize their attacks. After all, teams following a chain of command are far more effective than a single individual. The leader of a group of demons assigned to attack a victim is the prince; all the other demons, spirits, and curses below him constitute his kingdom. When I explain how to do a blind deliverance (expelling demons from a victim without using the gift of discerning of spirits), the importance of the prince and his kingdom will become obvious.

Demons do bad things. When we get rid of the demons, we also want to get rid of the effects of their presence. Therefore, we command them to come with "all works and effects," and we send them to the pit with all the bad stuff they did to the victim. After praying for deliverance, many people are healed immediately without even having to pray for healing, since sickness and pain are often the works of demons.

We learned much of what we know through trial and error. For example, we discovered that if we did not send demons into the pit, they might visit us at night or simply go to another victim. This has happened multiple times. However, when we send them into the pit, they depart permanently. We also learned that demons are legalists and will parse words in an effort to avoid compliance with your commands if it suits their purposes. For example, if you send demons *to* the pit, as compared to *into* the pit, they may actually go to the pit, look around, and then return to the victim. They may not depart permanently until sent *into* the pit.

I know there is some disagreement among deliverance ministers out there about whether or not demons actually go into the pit. Some say we should just bind them and command them to leave the victim, and that we can't send them to the pit before the time. I don't think the Bible speaks to this issue with certainty (thus the debate), but we do what we do on faith and it works, so we don't quibble about details. However, I do want to elaborate about the possibility of demons escaping the pit and returning to the victim following deliverance.

If the victim at a future time rejects and denies their deliverance, the demons can return. The losing combination for this type of failed deliverance is a demon of pride paired with a demon of deception. We have only seen demons return in the rare case of the presence of those two demons.

Other times, a demon seems to return; however, it is not the same demon but a repeat attack by a new demon with the same work. This can happen if the victim falls into the same problem that invited the demon in the first place. The original demons, however, are still defeated and bound in the pit.

Demons are soldiers following orders that are dispatched by superiors. If those orders are not captured, collected, and destroyed, other demons will take those orders and resume those tasks even after the originally assigned demons are expelled. Therefore, during deliverance it is necessary that we command the demons to collect all orders and take them into the pit and burn them. We may also ask angels or the Holy Spirit to do the work.

Angels and the Holy Spirit are our helpers during deliverance, and can be called upon at any time to assist with immobilizing demons, forcing compliance, and even disciplining them. Though demons and angels are spiritual in nature, they can receive blows and be burnt with fire in a spiritually distinct yet similar way to physical beings. Occasionally, the services of angels or the assistance of the Holy Spirit are necessary to force compliance. We always need them to bind the strong man, bind angels, gather and burn orders, and burn any objects associated with witchcraft.

As a practical example of deliverance, let's look at a person being attacked by a demon of defeat from a generational curse, disturbance from witchcraft, anger, bitterness, and a spirit of fear. Defeat is the prince, and fear is the gatekeeper.

In this case, the victim needs to repent and ask the Lord to forgive any sins of anger and bitterness; this can be done out loud or privately. They also need to forgive and release anyone towards whom they are bitter. Sometimes people want to repeat an appropriate prayer after you; this is enough to break the permissions of any demons.

Next, renounce the spirit of defeat and his entire kingdom, in Jesus' Name. Then you pray and declare:

I bind the strongman over (victim) in the Name of the Lord Jesus Christ. I bind the spirit of defeat with his entire kingdom. I break the generational curse of defeat in the Name of the Lord Jesus Christ. I break the curse of witchcraft in the Name of the Lord Jesus Christ. Holy Spirit (or angels), send fire and burn any objects associated with witchcraft. Spirit of Defeat, come forth with all works, effects, and orders. I bind you with all works, effects, and orders, with your entire kingdom, as one. Come as one. Go, now, into the pit, with your entire kingdom, with all works, all effects, and all orders. Burn the orders and lock the gate, in Jesus' Name, Amen.

Note that the demons and spirits did not need to be specified by name, but rather we can expel them as a group under their prince. The fact that they behave this way is very important when performing blind deliverance (deliverance without using the gift of discerning of spirits).

The powers of darkness are unrelenting. They will continue to attack no matter what. In order to remain free and victorious, the delivered person must be actively engaged and vigilant—more on maintaining deliverance later.

Blind Deliverance

Blind deliverance is performing a deliverance without using spiritual gifts. Since most Christians do not utilize discerning of spirits, this may be the most practical and actionable section on deliverance in this book. Herein I will describe exactly how it is done.

When we don't have the ability to see into the spiritual realm through gifts, we must instead interview the candidate to determine, to the best of our abilities, the most likely attackers. For deliverance to be successful, it is incumbent upon the candidate to be transparent and honest. After all, they are the only ones who know what they struggle with spiritually and emotionally.

When we conduct a first-time deliverance in preparation for baptism, we always start by performing a spiritual inventory. (An example may be downloaded at www.KingdomDriven.org.) For more details concerning performing a spiritual inventory or defeating strongholds, refer to my prior book *Christianity Unleashed*.

During this assessment, we identify sins, strongholds, generational strongholds, and areas of victimization. These categories encompass most areas of demonic attack, though not all. Strongholds are sinful or behavioral struggles or predispositions in our life which are difficult to break free from. Addictions, lusts, and other allegiances or activities such as cults or religions and occult involvement all can result from or lead to demonic permissions to influence our lives and future generations.

Some difficult-to-assess areas of demonic attack are the result of less obvious sins or may simply be the result of victimization: depression, doubt, fear, insecurity, unforgiveness, and worry are common. Scripture commands us to stand firm against all of these; a weakness in any of these areas may be taken advantage of by the demonic realm.

Even more difficult to identify are attacks such as defeat, disturbance, sickness, pain, division, weakness, and so on. These attacks are sometimes sent because of curses, and other times are simply the enemy's best attempt against us. Therefore, we must be attentive to all areas in our life that may be leveraged by the enemy. Have you ever just had a feeling that something is "off," but you can't put your finger on it? The demon of disturbance often works in that way, just trying to keep us off-balance. If a victim can identify such feelings or problems, even in a general way, this information can be used effectively in blind deliverance.

Here's a general rule for deliverance: *it is always better to expel a demon that is* not *there than to let one remain who* is. Therefore, we need to be as thorough and exhaustive in our evaluation as possible. Write down everything: sins, softer sins, personal strongholds, generational strongholds, areas of victimization, and all other miscellaneous potential areas of attack. Then confess and repent of sins, renounce all strongholds (personal or generational), forgive and release all who have victimized you, and finally renounce all demonic activity over yourself.

Now it is time for deliverance. If you are doing self-deliverance, pray through it. If you are taking someone else through deliverance, you lead the prayer. Pray this way:

I bind the strong man over [name] in Jesus' Name. I bind the prince over [name], with his entire kingdom. I bind the spirit with the highest authority responsible for: [name every sin, stronghold, or other challenge you identified during the spiritual inventory], and their respective kingdoms in the Name of the Lord Jesus Christ. Come as one, with all works, effects, and orders. I break and cancel all curses over [name] in the Name of the Lord Jesus Christ. Come bound as one, and go into the pit, with all works, effects, and orders. Burn the orders and lock the gate, in Jesus' Name, Amen.

If any resistance is felt in the process of expulsion, simply pray directly toward the spirits associated with the items on the list one by one. For example, if anger was an item on the list, bind the spirit of anger and command him to go according to the prayer detailed above. You will want to do this until the victim senses a release, freedom, and peace. Then pray for emotional and physical healing, and for the Lord to renew the person's mind, as detailed in the next chapter.

Brother Patrick and another evangelist brought six baptismal candidates in to Cindy and me for deliverance. They had already completed their spiritual inventory and repentance. Even though our evangelists are properly trained on doing deliverance blindly (without the gifts) by themselves, if we are around, nearly every evangelist field team still relies on us for at least a double-check. (And of course, to identify people's spiritual gifts, which can't be done blindly.)

On this day, they had not even attempted deliverance and just allowed us to do it using the gifts. We identified the demons, curses, and spirits of all six candidates as usual, and the team was shocked to see that everything mapped exactly to what they had written down during their spiritual inventories. We also explained that two of the people were already born again and did not require baptism. Again, to everyone's amazement, the report was perfectly accurate.

With this testimony, let the Lord be glorified as He distributes spiritual gifts for use among the Body. But also, be encouraged that blind deliverance based on an honest interview process can be an incredibly effective tool for successful deliverance.

Fighting for Freedom

After deliverance, the work is not over. Remember that the gatekeeper spirit is oftentimes associated with a soul wound resulting from emotional trauma. A soul wound is a spiritual injury to a person's soul. Much like a physical cut can subject someone to infection, a soul wound can subject them to a spiritual attack. If this wound is not healed after deliverance, it will simply attract a new spirit who will open the gate once again. Therefore, emotional healing is an often-overlooked, but crucial, next step after deliverance.

We discovered this when one day the Lord told us we were missing something important regarding deliverance. As we sought Him in prayer, He ultimately showed us that some of the people we had delivered were encountering repeat attacks because demons were attracted to, and taking advantage of, soul wounds. By luck (or Providence), I stumbled upon a very simple and effective teaching about emotional healing on YouTube, which led me to read a very short book about emotional healing by an author going by the pen name of Praying Medic. We immediately began identifying and addressing soul wounds following deliverance, which greatly reduced the recidivism rate.

I'll share the method we adopted based on what we learned. In order to identify wounds, ask the victim if they have any recurring emotional struggles that can be traced back to a traumatic event or deep hurt they can easily remember. It is great when they can recognize it, but sometimes they can't. If identified, take them through emotional healing. First, have them meditate on the specific event and describe the emotions they feel when they think about it. Then, simply pray that the Holy Spirit would heal the wound and close it off, rendering it ineffective as a future open door to demonic attack.

After praying, ask the victim to again think about the event and describe any emotions they feel. The negative emotions should be gone. If not, dig deeper and identify other events (perhaps related to the original) and other recurring negative emotions. Repeat the process for every traumatic or significant event associated with negative emotions.

This process of emotional healing is easily as amazing as physical healing. The resulting impact on the victim's life can be even greater. Do not underestimate the value of healing soul wounds.

Regardless of whether or not a soul wound is identified, post-deliverance prayer for wholeness, for the old to be replaced with the new, is helpful for closure. The demonic influence and its works and effects, when expelled, leave a void in need of filling. Lay hands on the victim and pray for God to fill them with His presence and power. Ask the Holy Spirit to go into their innermost parts and hidden places and bring healing: to their Body, to their soul, to their mind. Pray for the Holy Spirit to renew their mind and give them the mind of Christ. If a soul wound is identified, ask the Lord to heal their soul, make them whole, and heal any harm or damage to their soul resulting from trauma, in the Name of Jesus. Then pray for the Holy Spirit to fill them completely and activate their gifts. If they have any physical problems, this is when you will pray for healing; more on this later.

Once deliverance is completed, there is a need for counsel and encouragement so people know what to expect going forward. I said previously that a person, once delivered, needs to remain vigilant and maintain that freedom. Remember, the enemy never sleeps; attacks will continue and our job is to be alert to the enemy's schemes and remain victorious through prayer.

Deliverance should not be considered a complete defeat of the powers of darkness, but rather their temporary setback. When the bound (temporarily blinded) strong man recognizes that his troops (the minion demons) have been expelled and defeated, he will issue orders for a renewed attack. If the permissions are completely removed, then he will focus on opening the gate. Recall that gates are primarily opened through emotional trauma. Watch for it, pray against it, and don't take the bait. If the victim is weak in certain areas, specifically those attackers invited because of sin, the attack will likely be in the form of temptations, to get the victim to reestablish permissions for the enemy's work.

In order to stand firm against a renewed attack, bind the strong man daily. Pray that he will not issue any new orders. Pray that all schemes and plans will be exposed and defeated. Ask the Lord to send angels to collect any orders issued and burn them. Also, bind the defeated prince and each known member of his kingdom individually by name/work. Although the old bad guys are gone, the enemy knows your weaknesses. Demons are opportunists, seeking any vulnerability. If you bind them daily, those opportunities are circumvented. You are putting an impenetrable hedge around yourself. When you do this consistently for weeks, the enemy will simply give up on those areas and be forced to attack in a completely new way. You compel him to change his approach, because you are fortifying your defenses in your historical areas of weakness.

If the victim is weak, they may need intercessory support to maintain victory. However, if they are given to giving up easily or returning to sin, their deliverance will be in vain. Deliverance is not a silver bullet. The victim must make a commitment and follow through with it. For deliverance to succeed, the victim must believe, must want to be freed, and must be willing to fight to maintain their freedom. Others can't do it for them. However, intercession can help greatly.

Some are not willing, or able, to fight for even their initial deliverance. What about them? We all love and minister to people who would greatly benefit from deliverance, but they don't know it. They may be unsaved, may not believe in deliverance, or simply don't believe they need it.

We have limited permission when it comes to performing deliverance on uncooperative victims. However, that is not to say there is nothing we can do. By understanding the dynamics of demonic attacks and the fundamentals of deliverance, we have been able to achieve great things in the lives of the non-believing spouses and children of the saints here in Kenya. We have seen prodigal children restored, estranged spouses returned and saved, and other prayer targets redeemed. We have a lot of power through the use of basic spiritual warfare techniques.

Demons are permitted to disturb victims if they are invited because of sin. As I mentioned previously, we can't expel them from non-believers or people who are not cooperative with deliverance. However, we can consistently bind them. Simply bind the strong man and "the spirit with the highest authority" over any area of concern (unbelief, rebellion, addiction, etc.). Do this daily until you see the desired change in the victim. It will come. You must persevere in faith and believe that God will fight for them.

Any demons that are not sin-related can be expelled. Bind the strong man, break and cancel all curses, and bind and expel any demons related to curses or victimization. (This was covered more specifically in the previous chapter on blind deliverance.) Doing this may not get rid of the demons contributing to the victim's greatest vices. However, it will have a big influence on their mental and spiritual condition, and weaken the position of the remaining demons greatly.

When you are done binding or expelling the rogue spirits, follow up with prayers for the Lord to intervene. Ask Him to dispatch angels and fight for your prayer target. Pray for healing for any soul wounds. Pray for the Lord to renew their mind. Pray for the Holy Spirit to convict them of sin and bring them to repentance. Pray for the Lord to draw near to them and for them to draw near to Him. Do this daily until you see the desired results. Don't give up.

We all need to be active in the fight: to maintain our own freedom, to intercede for weaker brothers and sisters, and to contend for non-believers and help them come to a point of surrender to the Lord. Our fight is not against flesh and blood, but against the spiritual forces of evil in the heavenly places. Our weapons are not carnal, but are powerful for the pulling down of strongholds. Let us stand firm in the battle and we will see the Lord bring His victory.

Three Works of Front-Line Ministry

Jesus publicly entered the scene following His water and Spirit baptism and performed three specific works. Throughout the gospels, we see that He preached the kingdom, healed the sick, and expelled demons. I have already covered expelling demons, or deliverance, in great detail in the prior chapters. I will talk about healing in future chapters. I did not intend to focus too much on the subject of preaching the kingdom of God in this book because that should be an elementary teaching (though to many it is not). For more extensive teaching on the kingdom of God, I will refer you to two books, *Pioneering the Kingdom* and *Christianity Unleashed*. There is also a presentation on the gospel of the kingdom and other related teachings on my YouTube channel (Kingdom Driven Ministries).

For the sake of brevity, but so as not to neglect sharing vital information at this juncture, I will simply excerpt from my prior book *Christianity Unleashed* a brief description of what Jesus was teaching:

"So what exactly *is* the gospel of the kingdom? If this is the message that we preach when evangelizing, healing, and delivering the lost, it's essential to be able to share it with clarity.

If you ask someone what Christianity is about, the stock answer will be something like, "God's redemptive plan for humanity." But Jesus only mentioned dying on the cross for our sins a handful of times. He talked about our need to be born again just once. He discussed being sent as a ransom once. He only mentioned church twice. Yet the "kingdom of God" is mentioned about 100 times in the New Testament. You'll notice that most of Jesus' parables start with, "The kingdom of God may be compared to...," and then He tells a story.

Jesus said He was sent to Earth to proclaim the kingdom of God (Luke 4:43). What Jesus sent His disciples to do was exactly what He had been doing (Luke 9:2, Mark 4:23, and Matthew 9:35). Jesus explicitly stated that the end of the world would not come *until the gospel of the kingdom* was preached to all nations (Matthew 24:14). That is exactly what His followers proceeded to do after His death and resurrection (Acts 8:12, 28:23, and 30-31). In fact, the establishment of this kingdom on Earth was what Jesus commanded His followers to pray for (Matthew 6:10, Luke 11:2), and the culmination of God's work is the fulfillment of this prayer (Revelation 11:15).

In my opinion, the best passage to summarize the gospel of the kingdom is Colossians 1:13-14: "For He rescued us from the domain of darkness, and transferred us to the kingdom of His beloved Son, in whom we have redemption, the forgiveness of sins." In essence, we all start off as enslaved to Satan under the law of sin and death (Romans 5:12). Jesus was sent as a ransom to redeem us from bondage (1Timothy 2:5-6). Since Jesus never sinned, death was powerless over Him and He rose from the dead and conquered death

(Acts 2:24). Through repentance and baptism, we can partake in His death and resurrection (Romans 6:2-7); by His shed innocent blood, our sins can be cleansed (1 John 1:9). Therefore, when we die according to the flesh, death will likewise have no power over us and we will resurrect at the last trumpet (1 Corinthians 15).

How do we enter the kingdom of God? Quite simply, through water baptism and receiving the Holy Spirit (John 3:5). It would also be accurate to say that the kingdom enters *us* (Luke 17:20-21). However, entrance is just the first step—only *inheritance* is permanent. The branches, though they have been grafted into the Vine, will not all remain, except if they bear fruit (John 15:1-10). In the same way, unrighteous saints will certainly not inherit the eternal kingdom, in spite of having entered through baptism and receiving the Holy Spirit (1 Corinthians 6:9-10, Ephesians 5:5-6, Galatians 5:19-21).

Depending on your Christian background, perhaps these teachings are as foreign to you as they were to me at the time I was first exposed to them. Yet this is exactly what our New Testament teaches, as validated by the early church. The thesis is this: Christ was sent to redeem us from the domain of darkness, cleanse us, change us, and impart the Holy Spirit in us, such that we can abide in His teachings and bear fruit unto salvation. We are saved by grace through faith. We offer faith; He returns His divine power (grace—see Titus 2:11-14) to change us. Why? So that we can walk in the works He prepared for us to do (Ephesians 2:10), and so that by persevering in righteousness and holiness we will receive the promise of eternal life. (Hebrews 6:4-6, Hebrews 10:26-31, 2 Peter 2:20-22). This is the gospel of the kingdom preached by Jesus, the apostles, and the seventy. This was the gospel Philip brought to Samaria (Acts 8:12). This was the gospel that Jesus gave Paul on the road to Damascus (Acts 26:16-20). It was the very message Paul was teaching (Acts 28:23, 30-31). This is the revolutionary message that we need to understand to become effective in the front-line battle, because this is the message that must be preached as we go out as soldiers for the kingdom of God."

As already revealed in this excerpt, Jesus sent the twelve to do the same three works He Himself was doing (Luke 9:1-2). Then He sent seventy others to do the same (Luke 10:1-20). Elsewhere Jesus explains that these same works would accompany those disciples who believe (Mark 16:15-18). Therefore, these three works were never meant to be limited to special people at a special time. They were meant to be the normal Christian experience for all believers.

Healing Essentials

Healing may be considered a complicated subject. However, once one understands all the variables involved, it becomes quite simple.

When writing a Facebook post about healing, I said that all healings were not guaranteed because we are part of the equation. Later, I pondered whether or not healing could actually be described in equation form. Being a scientist with a strong math background, equations are how I best understand things.

This is what I came up with:

$$H_t = GP \times F_t - C$$

H = Healing
GP = God's power
F = Faith
C = Curses
$_t$ means with respect to time

A couple terms can be expanded further:

$$GP = GG + GW$$

GP = God's power
GG = God's glory
GW = God's will

And further:
$F_t = (FH_t + FP_t + FW_t)$

F = faith
FH = faith of the healer
FP = faith of the patient
FW = faith of the witnesses
$_t$ means with respect to time

So the full equation is:

$H_t = [(GG + GW) \times (FH_t + FP_t + FW_t)] - C$

This little equation accurately describes every example of healing (or failed attempts at healing) that I have encountered, and it is supported by quite a few Scriptures.

As you can see in the equation, healing is time-dependent. Though in the Scriptures every example of healing appears to be instantaneous and is presumed to be permanent, in the field we see many healed ailments recur an hour, a day, or a week after the patient's complete and often instantaneous healing. This apparent discrepancy may simply be because the Scripture authors documented events with no follow-up. If illnesses or injuries recurred, they may not have been around to see it. Or perhaps faith was sufficient for complete and permanent healing (an attribute that can be lacking today). One thing is certain: when we pray for healing today, some ailments are only temporarily or partially healed. Why?

The healing equation contains three main variables: God's power, Faith, and Curses. We can safely assume that God does not change in the midst of a healing. Though He certainly may respond to circumstances according to His will (and we can't always know His will with certainty), I can't imagine that He would change His mind about healing and cause it to be reversed. So the variables most likely responsible for recurring ailments are going to have to be faith and curses.

In the equation we see God's power is multiplied by faith to result in healing. His power can be greater or less and faith can be greater or less. If God wants to heal someone He can, even if faith on the part of the participants is minimal. He just exercises more power. But it is faith that releases God's power. If there is zero faith, all God's power will still result in no healing. And doubt is actually negative faith.

But whose faith is needed for healing? In Scripture we see three options: the healer, the patient, and witnesses. When the man asked Peter and John for money, the last thing he expected was to be healed. But he was, because Peter and John (the healers) had faith for his healing. There are many such examples in the Bible. But we also see Jesus healing many and saying that the patient had sufficient faith to be healed. Paul looked upon a man whom he saw had sufficient faith to be healed. The woman who was bleeding for twelve years was healed by simply touching the clothes of

Jesus. These people had faith for their personal healing. However, in yet other examples, such as the Centurion or the men lowering the patient through the roof, or the Syrophoenician woman—all were seeking healings not for themselves, but for someone else. In these examples, witnesses possessed the faith for healing.

So any faith will do: from the healer, the patient, or witnesses. Now when an experienced healer is praying for others and they are healed, oftentimes the patient actually does not expect to be healed and is amazed by it. They are healed completely because of the faith of the healer. This is where the issue of time comes in, because the cumulative faith at the time of healing is FH + FP + FW. FP is assumed to be zero, and let's say for our example that there are no witnesses. All the faith comes from the healer. So what happens a day later when the healer is not there? The patient himself needs his own faith to sustain the healing. As soon as any doubt sets in, the ailment can simply return. I have seen such circumstances but have had opportunity to pray again and encourage the patient in their own faith. The healing can then be sustained because the patient, having seen the ailment healed twice, acquires his own faith and in the future can release God's power to sustain the healing.

The second reason for recurring ailments or failed healings is when the ailment is the result of a curse. In the equation we see that God's power and our faith are independent of curses. That means that all the power to heal, plus a healthy measure of faith, can't result in a sustained healing if a curse invites the ailment to remain or recur. That's why all healings need to start with deliverance. In fact, I have seen numerous people healed, having never even prayed for healing, simply by performing deliverance. I covered deliverance and breaking curses in a prior chapter and will not treat that subject again here.

After deliverance from curses, we simply need enough faith, from anyone, to overcome the ailment. A big problem requires big faith. A small problem requires less faith. There are ways to manipulate the environment to increase the available faith. Remember, it doesn't matter who has the faith: the healer, the patient, or witnesses. And faith can increase in real-time. So if you have someone with multiple issues, pray for the simplest issue first. Or even break down a single problem into discrete parts. With piecemeal success the faith of everyone present will progressively increase, allowing you to tackle greater challenges.

Ask the patient if they sense improvement each time you pray. With progressive improvement, everyone's faith will grow, likely allowing you to complete even a difficult job. I personally stop after three attempts if no improvement is sensed, because repeated attempts without progress causes my faith to diminish, not increase. Therefore, more attempts will prove futile. However, if praying continuously does not diminish your faith, persist. Because all the prayers, and therefore faith, you throw at the ailment will cumulatively contribute towards healing.

Likewise, if you have multiple patients seeking healing at once, choose the easier ailments first. When those are healed, the faith of everyone in the room increases, allowing you to succeed with the more challenging problems. Faith is like a muscle. It needs to be strengthened through exercise. Once you succeed with a particular ailment, you will have sufficient faith to tackle similar issues in the future. If you ever fail with a particular ailment, organize other healers or intercessors to go and pray for the patient together with you next time so more faith can be applied to the situation. With the successful healing, your faith can increase such that you can do it alone in the future.

We have covered curses and faith. Now we will address the final variable, God's power. This is where we get to the nitty-gritty of why some people are healed immediately, and others slowly recover. But first we need to address the concept of healing from a spiritual worldview as compared to a materialistic worldview.

In the West, healing is a fiat miracle where measurable and testable healing has taken place, independent of natural processes or administering any forms of treatment. In most of the world where a spiritual worldview prevails, healing is when someone has a condition and then it is gone at a later time, regardless of how that recovery occurred.

Let me give you an example. In the West, if it rains, people attribute that to the temperature, relative humidity, and barometric pressure. In places with a spiritual worldview, people know that God made it rain. Who is right? Well, the latter is correct, of course. Meteorologists can only measure those three parameters. But it is God who determines their respective values. It is indeed God who makes it rain.

In the same way, our immune systems, nutrition, or medical, pharmaceutical, or surgical intervention are all tools God can use to heal our bodies. When a poor villager here in East Africa recovers from malaria after taking medicine, they come to church on Sunday and praise God (not medicine) for their healing. Even the clinic that we regularly use has as its motto, "We care, treat, and God heals." That is a spiritual worldview of healing. It's important to keep these two views in mind as we consider God's power in play upon the process of healing.

God's power has two variables. The first is to glorify Himself. He uses miracles to demonstrate His reality and power, and the truth of His message. Nearly every example of healing in the Bible is driven primarily by this variable. When Jesus, those he sent, or the Apostles performed healings, they were evangelistically engaging prospects. In fact, when Jesus sent out the seventy out two-by-two, he told them to heal the sick and declare, "The kingdom of God has come upon you." Just imagine how that would sound if people were not healed. They would have looked like fools! And certainly no one would have taken their message seriously. The purpose of healing was to demonstrate the veracity of the message and the power of the name they preached.

In such a circumstance, immediate healing is necessary. Otherwise, the prayer for healing serves little purpose. In fact, Jesus never did command the seventy to pray for the sick; they were commanded to *heal* the sick.

This phenomenon is exactly what I typically see in an evangelistic setting. During evangelism, people are almost always healed immediately. In fact, it is rare that someone is not healed during evangelism; though not all are completely healed, significant improvement is obvious and bears witness to God's power. Now let's compare this to ministering to the saints.

Because ministering to the saints is not exclusively for God's glory (for proving His power, presence, existence, or the veracity of His message), healing need not be immediate. After all, believers already believe. They know God is real, true, and powerful. Though the situation of praying for the healing of the saints is seldom covered in Scripture, it is inferred in several texts. The language used in the following passages describes healing more as a process than an event:

[14] Is anyone among you sick? *Then* he must call for the elders of the church and they are to pray over him, anointing him with oil in the name of the Lord; [15] and

the prayer offered in faith will restore the one who is sick, and the Lord will raise him up, and if he has committed sins, they will be forgiven him. [16] Therefore, confess your sins to one another, and pray for one another so that you may be healed. The effective prayer of a righteous man can accomplish much. (James 5:14-16)

[17] These signs will accompany those who have believed: in My name … [18]they will lay hands on the sick, and they will recover." (Mark 16:17-18 portions)

The terms or phrases, "restore," "raise him up," and "recover" suggest a process, not an instantaneous outcome. Though the latter passage is not limited to praying for the saints, the former is clearly such a reference. This matches my field experiences precisely.

A few examples of the saints being sick are documented in 2 Timothy 4:20, Philippians 2:25-27, 1Timothy 5:23, and Galatians 4:13-14. The passages imply they were all healed (except Timothy, who seemed to have a chronic ailment that was ongoing at the time of the writing), but they also suggest that the healings were not immediate.

With the saints, most are restored, are raised up, or recover. Immediate healing is far less common. That is not to say none are immediately healed, for this certainly happens. But recovery through process is far more common, as compared to the immediate healing seen during evangelism.

Now the second variable comes into play: God's will. Rather than for His glory, God's will may be to heal out of His love, mercy, and compassion for His children. God heals in response to heartfelt petitions and yearning for relief from physical ailments. God loves us and wants us to be freed from infirmity.

There are three mechanisms by which God's power can be unlocked: the authority of the Name of Christ, the power of the Holy Spirit, and God's compassion. Entirely different approaches are used to leverage each healing method. I will cover these in the next chapter.

Healing Practically

Though most may not appreciate a good math equation as much as I do, understanding the healing equation assists us in approaching ministry practically as well as theoretically.. Here it is again:

$$H_t = [(GG + GW) \times (FH_t + FP_t + FW_t)] - C$$

We've already gone through each component and talked about the necessity of delivering from curses in order to see permanent healing. However, there are some instances where a person can experience deliverance, go through healing prayer, and still not be healed. Why? In my experience, it can depend on how long the curse was active and how much damage the demons have done. A small problem requires small faith to correct. A big problem requires big faith. Therefore, all ailments *can* be healed. But healings are commensurate to the faith applied, or to God's power. It is necessary to increase one variable or the other in order to see progress in healing.

There are three mechanisms by which God's power can be unlocked: the authority of the Name of Christ, the power of the Holy Spirit, and God's compassion. Let's talk about how these three work and how to leverage them.

Jesus commanded his 12 disciples to heal the sick, and He gave them all authority over sicknesses and diseases (Luke 9:1-2). The same command and authority are inferred towards the 70 in Luke 10:1-19. Jesus said "these signs," including healing, will accompany all believers (Mark 16:17-18). Jesus commanded the apostles to make disciples and teach them to observe all He had commanded them, inclusive of the commands to preach the kingdom, heal the sick, and expel demons in Luke 9:1-2 (see Matthew 28:19-20). That means all believers were commanded to heal the sick!

When Jesus walked on the water in Matthew 14:22-33, Peter said to Him, "Lord, if it is You, tell me to come to You on the water." Now why do you suppose Peter would say such a strange thing? I'll answer with another question: what do you suppose would have happened if Peter had impulsively jumped into the water and walked towards Jesus? He most assuredly would have sunk like a rock.

Jesus responded to Peter's request with the simple command, "Come." And Peter walked on the water! Why was Peter capable of doing such an amazing thing? Because Jesus commanded him to do it! With the command came the authority. What happened when Peter feared and doubted? He sank. And then he appealed to Jesus, "Lord, save me!" That's when Jesus commended him for trying, right? At least he *tried* to walk on water; none of the other disciples did. Nope. Instead, Jesus rebuked Peter for doubting. Why did Jesus rebuke Peter and none of the other disciples? Peter was rebuked because he was *commanded* to come, and he did not. None of the other disciples had been commanded; thus, it was only Peter who was disobeying. Likewise, we are under command to heal the sick. How does our Lord view our failure to do so?

Another such example is in Matthew 17:14-21 when the disciples failed in their attempt to heal the lunatic. In that example Jesus firmly rebukes them for their failure to heal the patient.

The point I am attempting to make here is vitally important if you want to prove effective at healing. The reason Peter was able to walk on water, or the disciples to heal, is because they were commanded to do so. As soon as someone is commanded to do something, they are immediately given authority by the one issuing the command to complete the commanded task. Without the command, the authority is lacking.

This is why I have emphasized the fact that Jesus commanded the apostles to command successive generations of disciples to observe everything He had commanded them. Our belief in this, and all that it entails, is what grants us the authority to heal. And note why both Peter and the disciples failed in the two cases above: lack of faith. It is faith that activates the power granted by the authority of the Name.

I prayed for people to be healed for years with precious few actually being healed. That is, until I understood that I was commanded to heal and was, by virtue of the command, granted the authority to do so through the power of the Name of Jesus Christ. What happened when Jesus had to do the task for his disciples? He was disappointed with them for seeking His assistance. He expected them to do it.

Healing is a matter of tapping God's power, activated by our faith and through the authority of the Name of Jesus. Therefore, we do not ask God to do what He commanded us to do, at least not if we are invoking the authority of the Name of Christ. Instead, we command the sicknesses and ailments to go away. We renounce them and rebuke them. Sicknesses and ailments respond just as demons do to the authority of the Name of Jesus.

Let's say I have a patient with aching joints, fever, and a headache—classic malaria symptoms. Before we can utilize the first of the three healing mechanisms (invoking the authority of the Name of Jesus), we want to make sure curses are broken. Here is an example prayer:

I bind the strong man in the Name of Jesus. I bind the spirit with the highest authority causing this sickness. I command you to come with your entire kingdom, with all works, all effects, and all orders. I bind you as one. I break, cancel, and end all curses against the patient in Jesus' Name. Holy Spirit, burn any objects associated with curses. All of you, go now, into the pit, with all works, effects, and orders, in Jesus' Name. Burn the orders and lock the gate. In Jesus' Name, Amen.

With curses addressed, now on to healing—not by prayer, but by command. Pick the symptom you have the greatest success rate with and therefore the greatest faith for. Command something like this:

Headache, I renounce you in the Name of Jesus and command you to go, now. I command all pain, leave now. Go now, in Jesus' Name.

Ask the patient how the headache feels. If it is not gone, repeat similar commands until it is gone or until no progress is made following repeated attempts. I find that the more specific I am, the better my results. If it is a migraine, call it a migraine. If you suspect it is the result of constricted blood vessels, command blood vessels to open. Once the headache is healed, move on to the next symptom. If the symptom is joint pain, pick one joint at a time. After seeing a couple symptoms being healed in a row, there may then be sufficient faith, between you and the patient, to pray for (command) a complete healing of the overall or underlying cause of the symptoms. In this case, it is presumed to be malaria. That is how we heal invoking the authority of the Name of Jesus.

When Jesus sent out the 70 and commanded them to heal the sick and declare the kingdom of God was upon them, how many do you suppose healed the sick? I would guess all of them. Read their report in Luke 10:17, and ask yourself: how many of them possessed the gift of healing? It's a trick question—it was *none of them*! They could not have had the gift of healing, because the Spirit had not yet been sent nor distributed gifts to the saints. That occurred after Pentecost. They healed exclusively by invoking the authority of the Name of Jesus. But what about people today who do have the gift of healing?

Those with the gift of healing have been granted supernatural power by the Holy Spirit living within them to heal. They actually tap power granted to them, and do not simply invoke the authority of the Name of Jesus. It's a different mechanism, with the same end result: healing the sick.

Let us go back to our malaria victim for an additional sample prayer using the gift of healing. When I pray for someone to be healed (I have the gift of healing), I do exactly what was detailed above, but add additional prayers that tap into the Holy Spirit's power:

Holy Spirit go and touch their head now. Take away all pain. Heal all injuries or damage. Bring everything into order. In Jesus' Name.

Again, if you do not get results, always get more specific. Name the parts. I can give you examples of when I focused on the wrong parts and failed. But then when I narrowed in on the right parts, they were healed. One woman said she had a stomach problem. She was not healed. But when I determined it was a female reproductive issue and prayed for that instead, she was healed. Another complained of leg pain. I prayed with no effect. When I realized it was a nerve issue emanating from her lower back, she was healed.

The last mechanism for healing involves increasing the variable of God's power. God is moved to compassion by our intercession. Persistence and greater effort can move God to act on our behalf.

If today we encountered a lunatic such as we read of in Matthew 17:14-21, most of us would assume his condition was physical or psychological. Same with the woman with the bent back in Luke 13:11-16. Yet in both instances, a demon was the source of the problem. That is the reason we always start with deliverance. But we see that Jesus concludes about the lunatic, "This kind does not go out except by prayer and fasting." We can infer that some problems are bigger and require a bigger effort; more power can be applied to the situation via prayer and fasting.

In order to see the healing result we hope for, we can pray for a sustained period or organize a group so that many people can add faith to the equation. Intercessory prayer can get God's attention and prompt Him to release more power. In conjunction with prayer, fasting empties us of competing influences and can increase our faith. Both prayer and fasting, especially when it is part of a sustained group effort, can permit us to overcome challenges not otherwise surmountable.

When I visited America this year, several people were bringing patients in wheelchairs or in serious condition, expecting me to pray for them and for them to be immediately healed. They read the reports on Facebook of the paralyzed walking, and other amazing accounts. However, what they failed to understand was that those cases were sometimes evangelistic, where God did a miracle to spread the gospel. Others were the result of all-night prayer meetings with over a dozen intercessors, or after a period of fasting. These big problems were met with considerable spiritual resources and sustained effort. Any problem is surmountable, but some problems are big, and require a big effort to overcome.

You may not remember the healing equation, but you'll go far if you keep in mind the essential elements of success in healing: increasing faith, reliance upon God's power, and removal of all curses. Also, make a habit of commanding sicknesses and pain rather than praying to God to do the work. Start small and work up. Be as specific as possible. After prayer, ask if there is improvement. If a situation needs an increasing amount of God's power applied, turn to fasting and intercessory prayer. All Christians are given the authority to heal, so let's get out there and do the work!

The Revelatory Gifts

God is a living God who communicates with His people. He is not a mute object made of wood or stone that sits on a shelf. And He is not so indifferent to our affairs that He remains completely aloof or silent. He did not simply inspire the writers of Scripture a long time ago and then take a very long vacation, as some seem to presume. He is a person who knows us, loves us, guides us, and directs us. The revelatory gifts are some of the means by which God communicates with His people. Some of these gifts have already been discussed at length, such as discerning of spirits and the word of knowledge. Other revelatory gifts are prophecy, dreams and visions, word of wisdom, and tongues with interpretation.

With all the revelatory gifts, note that personal revelations about you given by others should only confirm the things God is ministering to you personally. Some information may be new and timely, but should resonate with you spiritually—what some might call an "inner witness." Accept what the Lord confirms to you. Disregard the rest until the Lord reveals more, either to support or refute it. The Bible says test everything, and hold on to what is good (1 Thessalonians 5:19-21).

Before I move onto the other gifts, I want to elaborate more about the purpose of the gifts already discussed. Understand that the gift of discerning of spirits is specifically to identify unseen spiritual entities as needed for ministry. The information is limited to what is beneficial for the entity being prayed for, be it an individual, church, or region. The information is meant to be actionable, and those actions are meant to be beneficial. Beware of anything that is shared with a spirit of judgment or for wrong purposes.

Words of knowledge are the Holy Spirit personally speaking to an individual. It manifests as our mind's voice, and can sometimes be difficult to distinguish from our own thoughts. The demonic realm works aggressively through demons of confusion and deception to distort reports. That is why we always bind the strong man and demons of confusion and deception immediately before seeking the Lord for any revelation.

Confident people typically get attacked with pride, leading to deception, whereas insecure people typically get attacked by confusion. Prideful people may confidently assert reports that are not true, while confused people either misunderstand or fail to act upon reports because of doubt. These phenomena are commonplace with all the revelatory gifts, but especially word of knowledge. This is because it is a very dangerous gift to the powers of darkness, permitting real-time communication with the Lord.

Word of knowledge is neither predictive nor prophetic. It is information for the present moment. Though some reports may be about things in the future, those things are changeable based on our response to the information provided. God often offers this information to move us in a particular direction, or to prompt action that can avoid or remedy an ominous report. Consider Isaiah prophesying to King Hezekiah about his imminent death. In response, Hezekiah prayed and the calamitous report was avoided. Isaiah prophesied accurately, even though the thing he said did not come to pass. The information was given to prompt a particular response.

As I said, the voice of the Holy Spirit via a word of knowledge can sometimes be difficult to differentiate from competing voices. Those competing voices are either demonic (confusion or deception) or even our own mind's voice. Binding the demonic can thwart their influence. Yet the Holy Spirit still has to compete with us. We must quiet ourselves in order to be able to hear from the Lord only.

A little exercise that works for me, and may work for others, is to eliminate other voices one by one. I start with binding the demonic as stated earlier. Then I ask in my mind, *are you there Lord*? You should receive an immediate *yes*. Any hesitation should make you suspicious. An immediate *yes* eliminates you as the competing voice. Next ask if Jesus is the Christ, the Son of God having come in the flesh. This should prompt another immediate *yes*. If that's the case, you can proceed with some confidence that you are hearing from the Holy Spirit.

Interestingly, some people actually hear God's voice in a distinctly different tone from their own mind's voice. With time and experience, your faith in hearing His voice will grow.

I write this with trepidation, because I am certain this can be abused if one so desires. However, this works for me. (And I believe it should work for all Christians since the Holy Spirit lives in us). With that said, it is prudent to confirm every report with another gifted person before acting on what you hear. Note also that all revelations will be timely and specifically for the benefit of the Body, and will not conflict with Scripture.

Word of knowledge is only slightly different from prophecy in that it is two-way communication. You can seek the Lord for guidance, and He can answer your questions. If you seek things outside your need to know, the Lord simply says, *that's not for you to know*, or something similar.

Prophecy, on the other hand, is God speaking only—one-way communication. For me, it has been declarative, and in the first person. The first time God moved with prophecy it was heavy. The voice was not the gentle voice of the Holy Spirit when receiving a word of knowledge. Rather it was loud, firm, and assertive. He was also speaking in first person clearly what He had intended me to say. It certainly got my attention.

I can't remember the words exactly, so I don't dare try

for fear of quoting God incorrectly. But I clearly recall the intent of the message. I was to declare in first person some terrible things an older brother had done, many in secret, for which I had no natural evidence. I was to declare his condemnation. I was to tell him to prepare his house because he would die soon.

I confirmed with Cindy that the report was indeed from the Lord. I was heartbroken. I loved this old man, flaws notwithstanding. I went to a private place and wept and begged for God to relent—to just give him one more chance, for me. And the Lord said emphatically, for the brother He would not, but for me He would grant one final chance. And then He told me the new message to declare to him: he needed to sell his most precious possession, repay all that he had robbed—four times the amount—and bring the balance to me for the benefit of the poor served by the mission. If he did not do this in seven days, he would die a condemned man. He came to visit me, and under the unction of the Holy Spirit, I declared the report in first person. First shock, then terror, then deep remorse fell over the man as he fell on his face, weeping bitterly. After he gathered himself together emotionally, he thanked me for the report, not refuting a single thing uttered, and left to do what the Lord had assigned him to do. Several days later, he returned with the money and restitution was made. He asked me to pray for him, and I did so.

Such an event happened with me only one other time. However, the Lord told me up front not to try to beg for this man, for he stands condemned and nothing could reverse it. His sins were too many and too great. I called this other old man and reported in first person his many serious offenses and told him to ready his affairs, because his death and condemnation were assured. He did not even blink; nor did he refute anything or argue the Lord's judgment. He left the church that moment never to be seen again, until his lonely death nearly exactly a year later.

This is how prophesy worked for me, likely because of my position of oversight and leadership of the mission. We have other gifted prophets among us, and any words from the Lord that they receive privately are typically shared with church leadership to get confirmation or to discuss any action that needs to be taken. Many words are given when we gather corporately for prayer or fasting, and they are publically shared and tested as received.

Note that as a rule, prophecy is for the edification of the Body (see 1 Corinthians 14:3). Under normal circumstances, the information is given to move the Body to action for its benefit. Therefore, if someone brings a valid negative report, accept it as an opportunity to bring about change through repentance or intercession; that is, unless the Lord specifically states that the outcome can't be changed.

Prophetic dreams and visions are another way that God speaks, either to an individual or for the benefit of the Body. These are, of course, visual messages given either during sleep or while awake. In our mission, many have this gift. Dreams and visions are very common during the quiet rest periods of all-night prayer meetings and during fasting. Typically a dream or vision requires some interpretation. As we have experienced it, the interpretation of a dream or vision usually comes from a different person, not the one who received it. Interpretation is a separate and unique gift.

Tongues can be a personal prayer language or can be used by the Holy Spirit to convey a direct message to the Body. In our mission, people are free to pray quietly in tongues during corporate prayer times when we are all praying out loud together. However, the gift of tongues and accompanying interpretation of tongues are reserved for proclamation to the group as the Holy Spirit leads.

Word of wisdom is the Holy Spirit unlocking and revealing deeper meaning into the Scriptures. This gift greatly compliments the gift of teaching.

In order to hear from the Lord through any of these revelatory gifts, personal consecration and elimination of distractions is necessary. Humility before God and others is also important in using the gifts as God leads, and specifically for the benefit of the Body. We also need to learn to listen attentively, both individually and corporately. God wants to communicate with and direct His people. We just need to make ourselves available for His communication.

Preparing for the Next Level

Our mission is very focused on discipleship, spiritual growth, and integrating all the saints into the work of the mission. We have learned that corporate fasting and prayer is the secret to advancing in power. This is because the Lord's presence is the means by which His power is unlocked. He will not remain close to those who are not close to Him. Intimacy with God comes by eliminating distractions and everything that displeases Him. Fasting is a way to get back to the basics.

The other secret to unlocking God's power is unity: common mind, love, spirit, and purpose (see Philippians 2:2). I see so many churches focused exclusively on the "one mind,"—that is, common belief and practice—but they neglect the other three. They lead with doctrine and set that as the litmus test for unity. Common belief and practice, however, are grossly insufficient to maintain unity such that a Body will have the stability and vitality necessary for God to release His gifts. Certainly common doctrine is valuable, but common love, spirit, and purpose are also necessary. Forcing common intellectual assent can actually invite unwanted spirits into the fellowship: pride, self-righteousness, division, and religiosity. However, if love and spiritual unity are the focus, the Body is free to seek truth and likely, with patience and humility, will find unity of doctrine as well.

Corporate fasting and prayer meetings (and also all-night prayer meetings) are great opportunities to draw the Body closer together in unity. The Body comes together, repents together, worships together, and prays together. Ideally, in a fasting and prayer setting, all distractions will be removed: home, family, work, phones, and any other forms of communication. Those who participate can experience a deeper level of personal consecration, which consecrates the gathering of the Body and invites God's presence. God will usually speak openly to His people, manifest His power, and unlock His gifts for the Church.

You may wonder, why fast and pray corporately, and not individually? It is because the gifts are for the Body—for the edification of the Body and for kingdom expansion. The Holy Spirit unlocks individual potential when that individual is in unity with a Body: one in love, mind, spirit, and purpose. Gifts are not for us, but for God to do His work through the church, and to expand the church, for Him. Those seeking power for the sake of possessing power need not apply. The power is for service, for God's good pleasure.

So what purpose is the one purpose? The church is not a social club; rather, it is an army. We are soldiers on a mission. That mission is to plunder the enemies and enlist more soldiers. Another aspect of the mission is to care for those in need, which shows God's love and can draw people into the kingdom.

In order for the Body to perform these works, individual activation of gifts and mobilization for service are indispensible necessities. Working as a

Body, with all the parts working in unison, is vital. When locals here in Kenya ask about our church, I always reply, "We are not a church; we are a mission." I wish every church could say the same. Viewing ourselves as one entity with one purpose mobilizes us to do the work of the Lord.

Approximately forty of the saints from about ten of our regional house churches met at our facility in the village for a two-day fasting meeting. This was a routine meeting that takes place approximately every six weeks. We had baptized so many new people at the time, averaging more than one disciple per day, that we were intent on helping the new believers draw closer to the Lord and see their gifts activated so they could be integrated into front-line ministry. Unbeknownst to me, it was not just the new saints that God intended to advance, but it was me also, and the entire mission. What He did next would test us all.

The Lord asked me if I wanted to go to the next level. I responded, "Of course I do." Then He said, "Get rid of your phone." I knew exactly what He meant. He asked again if I still wanted to go to the next level. I responded with all sincerity, "I don't know."

The Lord was not simply asking me to get rid of a handheld electronic device. He was specifically asking me to make a clean break with the support base of the mission. He was asking me to rely solely on Him and Him alone for the ongoing financial needs of our mission infrastructure. That was a tough pill to swallow and a heavy burden to bear. I could not make that decision without input from the rest of the church. Many of their livelihoods were at stake.

There was a time in my life when the Lord asked me to do something similar, in obedience to Him, and He came through spectacularly. However, it only affected me and my family. Even when becoming a missionary, I have made it my policy to not solicit money for my personal needs, nor do I take a salary from mission funds. My family exclusively relies on personal income from a rental property and unsolicited donations given freely by well-wishers.

However, when it came to others and to the mission, I have been quite free to solicit for the needs of our poor brethren and neighbors, and for the needs of the mission itself. When a patient needed surgery, or a brother had a funeral, I would simply post the report on Facebook and within hours the money would come. So this thing God was asking of me was going to affect me very little, but it would have a direct impact on the brethren around me. I could not just agree without first consulting them.

On the second day of fasting I reported what the Lord had communicated to me. I told the brethren that the Lord wanted me to get rid of my phone, Facebook, and all solicitations for funds for the mission if we wanted this mission to go to the next level. Instead of the anticipated shock or disappointment, the room erupted in cheers and shouts of joy. They were all elated that the Lord wanted to take us to the next level—that He wanted to provide for our needs directly, and not through my communications and solicitations. Two other prophets among us also shared prophecies that directly supported what the Lord had asked of me.

About a week before our fast, one of our prophets had reported three ongoing problems with our mission: fake disciples among us, money, and language. This major shift in mission paradigm stood to greatly influence two of those issues. As well, unbeknownst to me, several of our intercessors had met just three days prior for prayer and received a report that the Lord was soon to be implementing big changes in the mission. The Lord was definitely speaking to us and moving us in a very specific direction. Because the Lord was revealing His will to the entire Body, we were in agreement and unity. We knew that the changes would be difficult and that some would fall away as a result. However, we were confident that the sincere disciples would remain and a firmer foundation would be laid that would not fail.

Once we all agreed, I immediately began the arduous task of seeing where we stood financially and logistically as a mission. I looked at our regular income and regular expenses. I quickly saw a big challenge. Our regular expenses exceeded our regular income by a good $4,000. That difference was made up through some random gifts, but mostly through my direct solicitations and private messages via Facebook. So our leadership team, comprised of a board of six individuals elected by the church, would need to look at all of our regular expenses and cut the budget just about in half overnight. Ouch!

Of course, I could see the Lord's wisdom in all this. When I moved to Kenya, and for many years into the mission, it was always my earnest commitment to pioneer a sustainable and reproducible mission. However, things changed along the way. The first major change was when another family joined our mission with the intent of providing free medical assistance. Other ministries came alongside of us with business assistance and food. Since the funding was there, we simply expanded the scope of our ministry. However, this all had the very serious impact of local people seeing our church as a source of goodies from abroad. Though we did have many genuine disciples, the disingenuous also joined us. Even serious saints became discouraged about assisting each other, since we missionaries did everything for them instead. As our funding increased, our programs expanded. Our small mission slowly turned into an enterprise with a paid workforce.

On the evangelistic side, I had been the main evangelist, working with a translator, for quite some time. But as the mission grew, I trained and mobilized a committed group of field evangelists and we expanded the work. At first, no one was paid. But I quickly saw that we lost the best and most capable workers to secular employment, one by one. Since the unemployment rate is so high here, these people moved great distances, often to other missions which had much more funding than we did. Even those who remained with us still had needs, to support themselves and their families. So I began giving them an income suitable for their upkeep. And then there were government requirements for employees. Add motorbikes, driver's licenses, insurance, maintenance, phones, literature, and so on. In the end, even the evangelistic side required outside support. I prayed about this and the Lord burdened me to go full speed ahead with paid evangelists and teachers. The lost are dying in hordes; they need salvation. That is priority one.

However, these slow and steady changes in the mission, wrought through both circumstance and necessity, had unintended consequences. The mission was no longer sustainable and reproducible. Outside funding had become absolutely necessary for the mission to continue. The other unintended result was that I, Marc, had become indispensible, because I was the link to the outside world of funding.

I had always committed myself to minimizing my role. I always expected to pioneer something, train up others who could lead, and hand over leadership to them. So I take every opportunity I get to teach and encourage others to do everything I can do. That includes evangelism, healing, deliverance, teaching, church discipline, leadership, and everything else involved in managing a large mission with many moving parts. Contrary to some rumors I've heard out there, I am not a one-man show. That would be impossible. It's too big of an enterprise. We have layers of very capable people doing just about everything involved with running a dozen different Sunday services; numerous weekly bible studies; men's, women's, and youth meetings; prayer meetings; fasting meetings; discipleship; church discipline; feeding the poor and malnourished children; medical assistance; jigger treatment; evangelizing the remote villages; near-daily delivering and baptizing new disciples; maintaining our numerous vehicles; and performing a myriad of fiscal and administrative responsibilities. We are a team, executing these tasks with unity and precision. As now, when writing a book, I can make myself scarce for weeks at a time and the work continues. Praise the Lord.

However, there is one area in which I had inadvertently become indispensible and irreplaceable: fundraising. Aha! God saw the one area where I had become a potential liability to the long-term sustainability and reproducibility of the mission. So if God cut that link, the mission could survive and thrive.

As I write this, a brother visited my home to simply thank me for his medical treatment. He had fallen out of a tree and broken his back. He also had an ongoing problem urinating and required a catheter. Some time ago, we had solicited funds and he underwent the necessary treatments. Now he was able to walk to our home to thank us. He is the living, breathing reason why I answered, "I don't know," when the Lord asked if

I still wanted to go to the next level. Because when a huge need like that arises, I want to be able to help. In the past, that meant soliciting on Facebook or Messenger. But now my help is exclusively prayer. The Lord will have to urge people to give, absent my reporting.

Nearly at the same time as all these changes were underway, God had prepared us for a sudden and unexpected move back to the US. I won't go into details, but the message was urgent and the move seemed necessary. However, nothing could happen until after our new baby, Gideon, was born and received a passport, all of which was months out.

Upon personal fasting, prayer, and introspection I realized that the move was only necessary if I failed to make some personal changes that the Lord was speaking to me about. First, I needed to ignore my health and simply get to work. I had been suffering greatly from a couple ailments that would not desist and the result was that I was always giving in to how I felt. This made me far less active on the mission than I should have been.

Secondly, I was not to make this place my home. I had been sent to minister, not to colonize. During our tenure in Kenya, I had purchased two acres and three cows and started a very small dairy operation. Frankly, it was a disaster from day one. I had recently decided to reboot the farm with new fodder, new cows, and new workers. It was pressing forward when we suddenly thought we were returning stateside.

When I asked the Lord what to do about the farm, He responded that I should move full-speed ahead, because He was going to use the farm to support the mission in the future. So that is exactly what we have been doing. One day, on a future date known only to the Lord, this entire mission will be supported by Kenyan enterprise.

Meanwhile, with the necessary changes made, there is not currently a divine edict for our family to leave Kenya. However, eliminating the final role in which I am irreplaceable permits that possibility, if the Lord so directs in the future. Either way, we press on in the mission, tightening our belts to pursue only those essential tasks which the Lord funds. We prayerfully seek His miraculous provision when we are short for something absolutely necessary. We just keep doing the work.

All of this to say, we who labor for the Lord do so as a Body, each doing its part. As individuals and corporately, we must consecrate ourselves, seek His will, and move in obedience to what we hear. There is no limit to what God will do, but sometimes getting to the next level means making radical decisions and leaving behind places where we have become too comfortable. The risk is worth the reward.

Stepping into the Next Level

Cindy and I were praying for Michael, the young child of a local couple living on the farm I just mentioned. Michael was, for the second time in recent history, admitted to the hospital with malaria and pneumonia. His baby sister was going through ongoing illnesses as well. We weren't getting any answers about demonic influence or curses. This did not sit well with me. I knew there was something more to this family's health challenges.

I prayed specifically that any blocks or hindrances preventing us from seeing the source of his repeated illnesses would be lifted, and that we would see everything coming against him. And then we saw it: an angel of death and destruction, along with three demons: fear, disturbance, and death. But they were not simply attacking poor little Michael. The angel was a principality that was linked to the area, and specifically to their property. I performed deliverance and sent the three demons to the pit. This went without incident. But the angel was another issue. I knew we lacked sufficient authority to get rid of him. So I just prayed to bind him.

His presence was a mystery. I thought, *why would an angel have any interest in this remote rural property, and this little child?* Upon further inquiry the Lord revealed a clue: the name Tenochtitlan. A quick Google search of the name revealed that this was the place of Aztec ritual child sacrifice to receive favor from the "gods," such as rains in season. Then the Lord revealed that this angel was one of those "gods" of Kenya, having derived his power through the ritual sacrifice of children. Even more shocking, the property in question was one of those sites.

Though child sacrifice is, of course, not common in modern times, the angel continued to maintain his power through the bloodletting of circumcision, through animal sacrifices of tribal ceremonies, and through witchcraft practices. Another surprising, yet interesting, revelation was that the modern church practice of "sadaka," or offerings (also translated "sacrifice"), was likewise appeasement to him, and not an offering to the God of the Bible. Very often people give, and the church receives, to find favor—whether material blessings or protection—rather than out of pure motives such as returning gratitude to God or assisting the needy. Such is apparently a form of idolatry. This was a new and profound revelation to me.

Unsure about how to proceed, I was committed to learning what the Lord wanted us to do with this information. This angel seemed to be largely responsible for orchestrating the tragedy of common existence that defined life in rural Kenya: sicknesses, disease, death, and disaster are commonplace. Numerous funerals and countless serious ailments and accidents are the natural consequence of simply living here. This principality was the leader of an army of demons who personally plagued the masses with both spiritual and physical disturbances. This was a heavy burden. *What could be done?* I wondered. For the time being, I prayed to the Lord to bind the angel daily until He provided additional direction.

The Lord showed me the plan in a dream. I was in an office building with dozens of others I did not recognize. A man I knew to be extremely dangerous entered the room. Knowing he would recognize me, I made a hasty retreat with my son, Isaiah, in hopes of alerting the authorities before he saw me. At the main entrance to the building I saw that the door was fitted with a surveillance camera and rigged with an explosive device if opened. I immediately knew it was too late—we were trapped. Isaiah still pondered escape but I told him it was futile.

Moments later, the villain entered the foyer, brandishing a pistol, and forcefully escorted us to the board room with the other hostages. Alone with the hostages, or at least out of hearing range of the villain, I told them that attempting escape was futile because the he had rigged all methods of escape with explosive devices. I told them that by now the authorities were aware of our situation and we would have to await their intervention. The whole time I was encouraging the others to remain calm, I was thinking that if we rushed him all at once, only one or two would be shot, and we could prevail. But the risk seemed too great, and I considered that he might have some panic button that could activate a bigger explosion, so I did nothing to initiate a sudden revolt.

Meanwhile, one of the hostages panicked and made a hasty attempt to exit out the front door. We all heard a loud explosion, signaling her fateful and sudden demise. The rest of us took note of the gravity of our predicament.

The villain knew me and trusted me at some level. He knew I had attempted to advise the remaining hostages to be calm and cooperative. He saw that my leadership was an asset to his cause. He gave Isaiah and me the run of the building, knowing we would not attempt escape, and allowed us to sleep on furniture in the foyer while the others were cordoned off in the conference room. Eventually, he called Isaiah and me to join him in a small supply closet area and was very loose and unprotected with his pistol, brandishing it within my reach while looking away multiple times. Grabbing the gun crossed my mind multiple times but I restrained myself. Then he dropped the gun near Isaiah, just outside my reach, while he was several paces away on my opposite side. I looked at the gun and then made eye contact with Isaiah. I put my foot on the gun in front of me and slid it back to the villain behind me and told him he dropped his gun. As I turned to look at the villain behind me, I saw he had three other guns and was at the ready to shoot Isaiah or me if we tried to get the gun. As I suspected, it was a setup: a test of our loyalty. Of course, I was not actually loyal; I was just perceptive, and knew that we would not have prevailed had we retrieved the gun, which I now suspected was not even loaded. While he was behind me I could not stop thinking how close he was to me, and how easily I could grab his hands and call for Isaiah and the other hostages to tie him up and alert the authorities right outside to deal with him. But for some reason I did not.

We moved on to a kitchen area and I saw that the villain was the one preparing food for the hostages—actually, with great care. He even made special food for one hostage who had unique dietary needs. It was certainly odd, given his otherwise dastardly demeanor. He entrusted Isaiah and me to assist him. Then I woke up.

The meaning of the dream was immediately obvious. And the inferred plan of action was equally amazing. Through the dream, the Lord provided many valuable insights about this angelic ruler: he was shrewd, and in control. He had weapons we did not have. And we were unable to use his weapons. We could not destroy him. However, we could restrain him. The authorities who had far more power than he or us could destroy him, yet were forced to constrain themselves to prevent collateral damage. The strange and unexpected detail was the care he showed his hostages. He was bad, and dangerous, but oddly cared for his victim's needs. He knew if he was overly violent or antagonistic the authorities would storm in immediately. So he was biding his time—much how the demons temporarily respond with good things in exchange for offerings, appeasement in the form of sacrifices, allegiance, or worship. They bring bad things out of their inherent evil nature. But they bring good for their worship. They know they will be bound for eternity at the last day, so they are sure not to accelerate that inevitability by doing too much harm too fast, eliciting a commensurate response by the powers of good.

God and His angels can subdue or destroy any principality at any time. However, these rulers are holding humans hostage. They are close and armed and dangerous. To move quickly would bring sudden harm to many humans. So instead of going in guns a blazing, God needs us, who are in their midst, to launch the attack. We need to be prepared and ready to defend ourselves when we stir the bees' nest, because the counter offensive will be directed towards innocents, many of them unsuspecting.

The dream showed that there were three ways of subduing the enemy. One just mentioned: a full scale attack by the authorities. They indeed have the weapons and authority to either subdue or destroy the enemy. The second: overwhelm him with a mob advance. He may manage to inflict a few casualties as the multitudes attack him, but they will prevail. Then the authorities will take him away. The third, and best option: someone close to him restrain him by surprise and call for reinforcements. This was my answer.

The Lord revealed that this angel has ruled uncontested for over a thousand years. To date, no adversary has even identified him, let alone attacked him. He had a high degree of over-confidence in his invincible status. To identify him took a unique gift set. To defeat him would take a very thoughtful plan with a courageous group of warriors under able leadership. Only the perfect storm could knock him from his throne. He was very comfortable, presuming no one had the knowledge or courage to even try.

This angelic ruler was very aware of my presence and the rapid advance of our mission. We were delivering dozens from demons weekly, and sending his soldiers to the pit in so doing. We were healing the sick routinely. During the week of his defeat, we had baptized fifteen. Thirteen of us had embarked on a Luke 10, two-by-two evangelism mission right in his local village, where the gospel was preached to dozens and numerous were miraculously delivered and healed. This on the very day we launched our attack against him. He knew me. But he did not know I knew him.

The week I discovered his identity, I bound him daily. This simply means that he was partially restrained. As I said in a previous chapter, this is done through angelic means and the principality was not aware of my involvement. I also prayed daily that the Lord would mobilize an army of angels to fight the principality.

I scheduled an all-night prayer meeting for the following week. Isaiah and I fasted the day of the attack. I did not tell our intercessors the reason for the meeting, so as not to alert the angelic ruler of the intended attack. I only told Joseph, one fellow elder in our mission, the details.

When I shared the information about the principality, Joseph was not the least bit surprised. He told me some history about the region: about tribal practices of circumcision, blood sacrifice, demonic covenants, and about blood-letting in the area when it was still a forest and yet to be developed. He supported in the natural all of the supernatural insights we had received. He also told me about a head-to-head he once experienced when challenging a principality from another tribe. The principality was not defeated, yet it inflicted no harm to him either—call it a truce.

Joseph agreed we go for it: we attack Thursday night—the entire prayer team. As the day neared, the Lord provided me more and more confidence of victory, but it might not be without casualties. The Lord told me exactly how the attack would unfold, which gave me a clear blueprint of how I should instruct our intercessors to pray. He likewise made it clear that only I could do this. Only I had the authority. That is, apostolic authority. This angelic principality ruled the area. However, I was sent by God to this area to usher in God's kingdom reign. Apostle simply means "sent one," or *missionary* in modern English. Those sent by God are His emissaries, granted authority to assert His rightful rule in the place sent. So I had the vital role of launching the attack. This I had been doing secretly for a week by binding him, but now all would be made public at the all-night prayer meeting.

The Lord showed me that the angelic ruler would immediately solicit assistance from his satanic cohorts. They would rally to his aid in order to prevent his capture by the Lord's host. The armies of Heaven would need to overwhelm his defenses to get to him.

The scenario reminded me of Daniel chapter 10, where the angel dispatched to help Daniel was detained for three weeks until Michael intervened and overcame the Prince of Persia. I knew we wouldn't see the victory right away. In addition to soliciting angelic support, the principality would also unleash a "hail Mary" and dispatch orders to hundreds of demons under his charge to wreak all kinds of havoc upon us human attackers. These orders needed to be intercepted and destroyed. We would need to remain vigilant, possibly for weeks, against demon attackers who might get through, and follow up with deliverance for any of our people affected. I fully expected orders of death, destruction, defeat, disturbance, and every form of evil imaginable.

Such an endeavor is not for the faint of heart. However, the alternative is unacceptable: innocents needlessly suffering at the whim of this principality and his evil army. Once we began our prayer counter-offensive, the risk of harm would be immediately diverted from the innocent masses to the Christian soldiers. It was a chance worth taking. But would our intercessors agree?

The rains were unrelenting. Our intercessors trickled in from all over the area, many traveling great distances by public vans and motorcycles in the rain. At 8 PM we loaded two cars with those who had convened at my home. When we arrived at the meeting location, we realized that our team of 35 intercessors was more than could fit in the small mud-and-stick home. Several sat on chairs or stood in the doorway of the house.

At about 9 PM, I asked Joseph to open the meeting with prayer, songs, and a time of corporate repentance. Not until then did I explain to these 35 soldiers what lay ahead. I detailed the revelations and history concerning the angelic ruler. I explained the risks of action, inaction, success, and failure. I explained the extent of our authority over angels, and how we must call upon God and His angels to intervene on our behalf. I explained how the angel would recruit help to delay his defeat. I told our team that the angel would issue many orders for demons to attack us, this prayer team. And that the demonic attack might be sustained for weeks. I finally ended with the fact that we could experience casualties. This was not a game.

With that, I gave anyone who had fear, doubt, or worry about what I had explained or what we intended to do, the freedom to leave. As expected, none took me up on the offer.

After one powerful Swahili song specifically about spiritual warfare, we unleashed a torrent of fire and fury in prayer. For one uninterrupted hour we labored in unison and entered into serious warfare. We prayed God would unleash his army and subdue the principality. We prayed God's army would break through his ranks. We prayed the enemy's army would get confused and break rank. We prayed God's army would overwhelm and instill fear in the angel's army, and that they would retreat. We prayed all outgoing orders would be intercepted.

We prayed God's army would not relent, and would apply sustained, substantial pressure on the angel until he was permanently subdued. We prayed the Lord would put a hedge of protection, angels posted, over each and every intercessor, their families, and their properties. We pled the blood of Jesus over the property so that the innocent blood historically spilled would be redeemed from the idolatry. We prayed for the souls of the innocent children lost. We prayed, prayed, and prayed some more, until we were hoarse, sweating, and exhausted.

After I felt a release, the Lord granted a preliminary report, in addition to what I had sensed during prayer. The angel was completely ambushed—taken totally by surprise. As a result, his response was not very organized. He did have other fallen angels assist him, but they were quickly overwhelmed and turned on him or retreated when they recognized their defeat was imminent. They were not about to go down with that ship. Many attack orders were released, but only dozens, not hundreds. Most were intercepted and destroyed. And the best news: he was on the run, and unable to launch a coordinated attack on us intercessors. The lines of communication were broken and his forces were in confusion. The final report was that he would be subdued in just days, not weeks, and would be on the run until then. Mission accomplished. God wins again! God be praised and glorified.

We had no idea what we were getting into when we sought "the next level." Part of it was a step of obedience and a step out of our comfort zone, and another part of it was going on the spiritual offensive and taking on a new level of enemies. God was faithful to lead us, speak to us, and show us how to fight effectively. After our prayer meeting, the family living on the property both felt and saw significant breakthrough. We were all confident that much had happened in the spiritual realm, and that God had won the victory.

Spiritual Warfare

As our mission advanced to the next level, both in terms of God-reliance and spiritual warfare, a separation of the chaff from the wheat among our people was necessary. The level of consecration necessary for the Lord's service and the need for unity meant that we could no longer be a mixed group: those seeking material assistance and those seeking the Lord.

Two activities that have always separated the spectators from the soldiers have been prayer and fasting. And when I say prayer, I mean all-night prayer meetings, called *kesha* in Swahili. The word *kesha* means to watch, or be alert. This word is commonly used in Scripture in reference to spiritual warfare. It is not the faint of heart who sacrifice sleep to pray all night in a malaria-endemic region. That takes dedication. And these meetings normally attract thirty or forty people.

Our group meetings in Kenya are lively and engaging. They are always launched with many praise songs, followed by a worship song or two. Corporate prayer or fasting meetings start with personal repentance. For the Lord to hear and respond to our requests, we first must remove anything that separates us from Him. Each and every attendee draws near to the Lord, confesses sin before Him, asks for His forgiveness, and commits to walking according to His will. This invites the Holy Spirit to freely reign over the remainder of the meeting.

The powers of darkness are not threatened by spectator Christians. They do not fear good works, either: feeding the poor, medical care, offering business or financial assistance, or providing people with education and training. Even Muslim-majority countries can permit Christians to do those works with little interference. However, if you get active doing the three works Jesus modeled and taught (evangelism, healing, and deliverance in His name), you will have a fight on your hands. Those are the ticket to open warfare.

Therefore, once we step out in these things, we need to be armed and ready to fight back. And that fight is spiritual, not carnal. We need the tools and weapons of warfare to successfully combat the spiritual powers of darkness. Having sound doctrine and orderly meetings will not cut it. We need spiritual gifts.

Some of the gifts are revelatory and can help us learn of the enemy's plans and receive orders from the Lord. These include prophecy, discerning of spirits, word of knowledge, tongues with interpretation, dreams and visions, and so on. Others are for strengthening and empowering the troops, such as teaching, word of wisdom, and the practical gifts for church order. Still others are for open warfare such as faith, miracles, healing, and evangelism. They are all needed in the battle against the enemy.

However, the gifts don't operate in a vacuum. They are for the edification of the Body. They are distributed individually, but for corporate benefit. Therefore, it is during these corporate meetings we seek and hear from the Lord. On the other hand, we rarely receive revelations during Sunday service. I presume this is primarily because there are no breaks of silence, rest, and introspection as during the prayer and fasting meetings. Sunday gathers are busy from beginning to end. Likewise, we have a mixed crowd of spectators and soldiers in our Sunday gatherings, whereas it is mostly the committed that attend the prayer and fasting meetings. When we gather at the corporate events, the Lord guides us and corrects us. He gives orders and we receive them. He directly communicates with His people.

Fasting meetings are designed to eliminate distractions, bring us into unity, and draw us close to God. Then we are in a prime position to receive His revelations as a Body. In this way the church becomes more than just a church; it is a mission.

In addition to regular prayer and fasting meetings, we have a corporate teaching and prayer meeting every other Saturday. On alternate Saturdays we typically organize open-air meetings near where our fellowships meet or where we hope to plant new churches. We have weekly meetings for youth, women, and *wazee* ("old men"). Most meetings draw a mixed crowd of visitors, spectators, and soldiers, so we rarely receive revelations or see the manifestation of many spiritual gifts. However, these meetings gather saints from all of our regional house churches to one location, which facilitates unity even though we are separated geographically.

Lastly, we have organized daily prayers for the mission. Different house churches volunteer to pray for the mission each day. They organize in groups and pray individually on their assigned day to ensure that the mission has an around-the-clock prayer covering. Now I will share what we pray for. We are a mission, not a church. We send teams out daily doing Luke 10-style, two-by-two evangelism. They travel great distances on dangerous roads, rain or shine. Their motorbikes share the roads with cars, big trucks, other motorbikes, animal carts, all kinds of animals, bicycles, tractors, and pedestrians. The rutted dirt roads turn to slippery mud when the daily rains come in season. We pray for safety; that our evangelists will find and engage a "man of peace;" that people would be receptive to the message; and that these initial contacts will, in turn, engage their neighbors, friends, and family with the gospel message.

We pray for all our churches: for unity of love, mind, spirit, and purpose; for steadfastness and maturity; and for protection from authorities, wolves, and principalities. We also pray that our people will be active in the Lord's service and that they would reach out to neighbors, family and friends so that the kingdom will expand.

We also pray for our disciples: for God's protection and provision, for health and safety, for their spiritual growth (including the activation of spiritual gifts), and for engagement in the mission. We know that in order for these prayers to be most effective, we must bind the strong man and the spirit with the highest authority affecting each disciple (this is, of course, done in a general way). We bind all principalities over our fellowships and also break any curses against individual disciples.

We pray for the mission: binding all principalities over each ministry region, praying for the leaders and asking God to meet the financial needs of the mission. We ask for God's wisdom and direction. We also pray for our ongoing meetings (especially the open-air meetings and the weekly church gatherings), and we pray for all the different ministries and teams (feeding, medical, jigger removal, etc.).

A church is only as strong as its prayer covering. If you attend a church, fight for its leadership, the people, and all its work in prayer. Even better, participate in corporate prayer or help organize such prayer meetings.

Now I want to explain some important points about regional spiritual warfare, which I touched upon in the last chapter, to ensure that nothing is missed. Principalities are regional leaders loyal to Satan. They can be fallen angels or high ranking demons.

Christians have complete authority to defeat demons and send them to the pit, if they attack someone. Under normal circumstances, principalities give the orders but allow lower ranking demons to do the dirty work. Principalities have authority to reign in a region because of the propensity of the people in that area to be active in their area of specialty or assignment. Let me give you some examples.

In our area, the principality used to be jealousy/witchcraft (one demon, two linked works). We were here for five years before we defeated him. It was not until many people had repented of jealousy and witchcraft that we were able to prevail. Prior to that, he was firmly entrenched, here by invitation of the numerous people given to those sins. At the proper time, God made known His will for us to defeat this principality, and we prevailed in prayer. We did not send him to the pit, but rather simply displaced him from the area, since we were not performing a personal deliverance in which he was personally attacking a saint. Since this victory in prayer, we have seen major changes in the community as regards jealousy and witchcraft. Although neither can be entirely defeated, both have reduced substantially.

Believe it or not, in the end, we learned that our ability to displace this particular principality was not predicated on the large group of intercessors we gathered for the multi-day fasting meeting. It was based on apostolic authority. I, being sent by the Lord to the area to promulgate the kingdom of God as His emissary, was granted unique authority over him. This area was being commandeered for the Lord. His reign came to an end at God's direction.

In his stead, a new principality now rules. His work is intrigue (gossip, slander, and listening to gossip). With my newfound boldness, having seen jealousy/witchcraft defeated, I wanted to push him right away, too. The only problem is that he is firmly entrenched because he has many willing subjects in our village. In such a case, our only recourse is to bind him.

When binding a principality, daily ask the Lord to send angels to bind him. Ask them to gather all orders he has issued and collect them and burn them. Bind him daily until people change sufficiently to diminish his power over the area. When his power is sufficiently reduced, at the proper time directed by the Lord, you will be permitted to defeat him.

Remember, if you know or suspect that a higher-level principality or power is an angel, you do not have authority over him. You must petition the Lord to send angels to fight for you. And when they are defeated, they are simply reassigned, and forced to abandon their regional rule. Regardless, they are gone. Know that the sudden reprieve is not really a reprieve. The demons he ruled over are still there; now they simply lack command and control. They will likely continue their work, albeit in a disorderly manner. However, demons can, of course, be defeated and sent into the pit one by one. You can expect that at some point, the power vacuum will be filled by a new principality, likely of lesser rank and power. And the fight continues.

Note that principalities exist over nations, regions, communities, and even churches. Pray in earnest for the Lord to reveal who they are. If you don't get the answer, do it "blindly," which is observing and thinking it through. It should be obvious who these powers are when you identify the prevailing spiritual challenges over the area or group for which you wish to intercede. Bind these things daily to bring change in the people and in the area, until the principality's control is diminished sufficiently to defeat him.

The defeat of a principality should bring a certain level of spiritual freedom to an area. This will affect individuals, families, churches, and even government. Non-believers will be more open to the gospel, believers will be free to find freedom from strongholds, and an oppressive government may become less restrictive. Exercise caution when advancing in warfare prayer, being mindful of your sphere of influence and authority in the spiritual realm. I believe such prayer is better done corporately, rather than individually. God and His host, moved by your prayers as you bind and loose in the spiritual realm, will bring the victory.

As we advance, so also His kingdom advances against the spiritual forces in the heavenly places. It is both amazing and humbling to know that the Lord uses us to accomplish His plans and purposes in this place.

Where to Go From Here

As I have pursued the Lord in my personal walk and in the ministry, I have learned that He has pursued me more. Each and every extraordinary step we take together on this mission shocks and amazes me. And it is only a matter of time before the cycle repeats itself and He brings me to new places that I did not know existed. Our God is amazing. His wonders are magnificent. He wants to give us more than we know, more than we ask for or imagine. The question is, are we willing? Will we ready ourselves by eliminating distractions and everything that diverts our undivided attention from the Lord and His will for our lives?

In my experience, God's power is predicated on corporate unity. I am in a position to promote that unity in our mission, but many people reading this book will not have the authority or ability to make decisions on behalf of their churches. However, you can redirect *you*. Are you willing to commit to prayer and fasting personally, as described in this book? Your first prayer target would be to raise up intercessory partners. Then you and your partners can pray for an intercessory group. Then the intercessory group can pray for the church. Then pray for your church to become a mission: to reach your community, your town, your state, and your nation.

The church is one Body with many parts; be a peacemaker and a person of unity. Communicate with others in the church and with your pastor. Pray for the spiritual gifts to be given to the Body, and see how you can participate in the life of the church. The work of the church (which is the people, not an organization) is not to invite spectators or simply offer programs; it is to mobilize soldiers to do the three works commanded by Jesus: preach the Kingdom, heal the sick, and cast out demons. Our goal should be to advance beyond the elementary teachings and get to the next level that God has for us, so that His kingdom will come on Earth as it is in Heaven.

About Kingdom Driven Ministries

Kingdom Driven Ministries, Inc. (KDM) is a registered 501(c)3 ministry founded by Marc Carrier and his house church brethren in Indiana in preparation for East Africa mission work. The mission serves rural East Africa through evangelism, discipleship, church planting, feeding the hungry, medical missions, clean water projects, jigger treatment, and other vital needs. The mission upholds the historic kingdom paradigm of the early church and emphasizes obedience to the teachings of Jesus Christ.

KDM sends evangelist teams almost daily into the villages, seeking out the man of peace and teaching and baptizing new disciples who ultimately form into home fellowships. The churches and mission work are overseen by a biblically-qualified and ordained team of elders and deacons, comprised of both missionaries and indigenous saints.

By the leading of the Lord, the mission recently adopted a strict policy of not soliciting support from foreigners. However, this in no way means that the needs are not there. It just means that we can't ask for assistance from anyone other than the Lord. The long-term goal is to eventually wean off all foreign support by developing local sources of funding. The primary source that the Lord is currently leading us to invest in is a dairy farm, which includes tractor services for our farming community. It is a slow and steady, long-term venture. Meanwhile, if the Lord leads you to participate in this mission (either Great Commission or Great Commandment works) through ongoing support or a one-time gift, visit www.Kingdomdriven.org/donate. And if you wish to boost our mission's progress towards self-sustainability by investing in the farm through either a cow purchase or purchase of a tractor implement to diversify our services, donations can be earmarked as such with a note. Checks made out to Kingdom Driven Ministries may be sent to: Kingdom Driven Ministries, PO Box 1751, Martinsville, IN, 46151.

If you need assistance with personal deliverance (although we do ask that you try self-deliverance first), and if you want to identify your spiritual gifts, I encourage you to set up an appointment with Cindy and me. However, you will need to be patient. There is a big demand and we only take one call daily.

Lastly, if you are part of a leadership or intercessory team and would like us to help you identify the principalities affecting your ministry area, feel free to contact me.

Find me at Marc@KingdomDriven.org
Follow me on YouTube at Kingdom Driven Ministries

Made in United States
North Haven, CT
01 July 2023

38463362R00067